BARISTA COFFEE

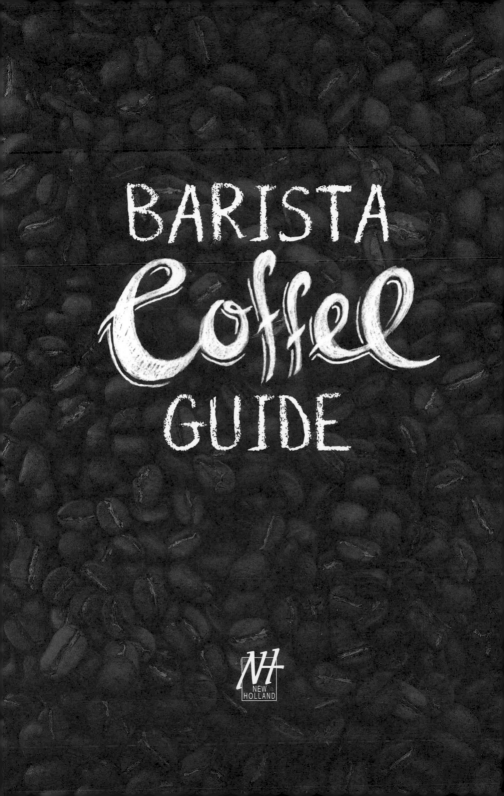

BARISTA
Coffee
GUIDE

NEW HOLLAND

First published in 2010 by New Holland Publishers
This edition published in 2021 by New Holland Publishers
Sydney • Auckland

Level 1, 178 Fox Valley Road, Waroonga, 2076, Australia
5/39 Woodside Ave, Northcote, Auckland 0627, New Zealand

newhollandpublishers.com

A record of this book is held at the British Library and the National Library
of Australia.

ISBN 9781760794156

Group Managing Director: Fiona Schultz
Publisher: Fiona Schultz
Designer: Andrew Davies
Cover Design: Yolanda La Gorcé
Production Director: Arlene Gippert
Printed in China

Food Photography: Paul Nelson, R&R Photostudio
Food Stylist: Lee Blaylock
Recipe Development: Michelle Finn, R&R Test Kitchen
Barista: Mitch Faulkner, Barista Trainer, Retail Food Group Limited

Special coffee roasting images by ESPRESSOLOGY *Coffee Roasters for
Expert Baristas*

The publishers would like to thank the proprietors of Tre Espresso Bar
of 459–475 Sydney Road, Brunswick, Victoria for their assistance with
photography of their espresso bar for this book.

10 9 8 7 6 5 4 3 2 1

Keep up with New Holland Publishers on Facebook

 facebook.com/NewHollandPublishers

@newhollandpublishers

US $16.99

Contents

Introduction

Coffee is one of the most traded commodities in the world, second only to oil. Coffee is grown in over 50 countries throughout the world, with many of those economies dependent on this great commodity.

In this book we instruct you on how to become a "coffee artist", through our pages of coffee art instructions, together with some great recipes for coffee cakes and biscuits.

Now you have your own coffee machine you can start to use it like a barista.

The process of preparing and serving espresso-related beverages seems, to the average person, a relatively simple task. However, as you start to use your machine you will find, initially, that the production is anything but simple. In fact it is a rather complex matter and will require a good deal of practice. Learning to extract café-quality espresso from your machine is like learning to shuffle cards – it takes practice but once the skills are obtained you will never look back.

You will notice that we refer to "crema" a lot in our instructions. You may innocently ask, what's that?

Crema is the heart and soul of espresso. Crema is the creamy, golden brown extraction that develops in the filter holder and settles at the top of your espresso serving. Delicate oils in the espresso grind form colloids (very fine gelatin-like particles with a very slow rate of sedimentation). Crema is evidence that the correct amount of fresh coffee was ground to the proper consistency, and the precise amount of water at the correct temperature was quickly forced under pressure through the fine espresso grind.

The history of coffee

Not many people know the mythical tale of how coffee was first discovered. Back in the 9th century, Kaldi, a humble Ethiopian goat herder observed how his goats danced and pranced about after eating the red berries of what we now know as the coffee plant. Amazed by the excitable behavior of his herd, Kaldi collected some of the magical berries and consulted a holy man who cast them into a fire.

The aroma produced by the roasting beans was so intoxicating that they were quickly retrieved, ground up and infused into hot water: history's first cup of hot coffee!

Since then, coffee has been the drink of choice by practitioners of political intrigues, social uprising and creative thought. Just how did the humble cup of coffee come to be ringside at the great shifts in cultural history in the West?

Coffee came to Italy from the Ottoman Empire during its thriving trade with Venice in the middle of the 17th century and the inaugural Venetian coffee house opened its doors in 1645. It took an Italian to establish the first café in Paris where, over mugs of hot coffee, Voltaire, Rousseau, and Diderot developed the philosophies that would give birth to the French Enlightenment.

Coffee houses soon spread like wildfire across Europe and became a focal point of social interaction. By 1675, England had more than 3,000 coffee houses. Authorities feared that such places encouraged political dissenters to gather, drink coffee and muck-rake the current monarch. Indeed, coffee drinkers at the oldest coffee house in London were implicated in plots to assassinate William III. Yet it was the same London coffee house that started listing stocks and commodity prices and evolved into the London Stock Exchange. Auctions held in coffee houses during the eighteenth century also laid the groundwork for the great auction houses of Sotheby's and Christie's.

By 1901, the first espresso machine was patented, which forced boiling water and steam through ground coffee and into the cup. Unfortunately, the high heat of the water gave the coffee a burnt taste, but, by World War II, piston machines replaced steam and kept the water at the optimal temperature. Because a lever was pulled to produce the coffee, it was colloquially called "pulling a shot".

By the 1960s, pump-driven machines replaced manual pistons and became standard in espresso bars. At the same time, coffee bars were becoming venues for counter-cultural performances by beat poets and folk musicians of the like of Bob Dylan and Joan Baez.

Coffee drinking took on an entirely new face in the 1970s and 1980s with the explosion of coffee bar chains into popular franchises. Such bars prided themselves on high-quality beans and superior equipment to produce an excellent standard of coffee.

By the 1990s, consumer espresso machines brought café-quality coffee into the home. Such machines sported a high-voltage pump that generated excellent crema and a wand for steaming and frothing milk, making it possible for consumers to produce a cup of espresso of equal quality to those made on commercial machines.

Getting Started

First you have to decide on the coffee
maker you wish to use. There are a number
of very good domestic appliances available,
and we will leave it to the professionals
in your favourite retail store to discuss
the attributes of each, allowing you to
make a decision that will fit your coffee
needs. Secondly you must also buy the
best grinder to ensure that the coffee
is ground correctly and will not burn.
Last and certainly not least, you will need
to experiment with coffee blends to ensure
you have the desired beans and roasts to
give you satisfaction.

Creating the Perfect Espresso:

The Four Ms

"Espresso" has become the shorthand for "caffè espresso", the beverage produced by forcing hot water through finely ground coffee. It is this process that creates the elusive crema – the intense, silky layer of orange-brown foam that is the signature of an espresso coffee.

It is said that making the perfect cup of espresso coffee requires the four Ms: Miscela, Macinazione, Macchina and Mano.

MISCELA
– THE COFFEE BLEND

Coffee blends can be chosen for a number of reasons: to create a signature blend, to balance the aromatics of different coffee species, or to capture the purity of coffee from a particular coffee-growing region (this is known as single-origin coffee).

Arabica or Robusta – what's the difference?

The two most important species of coffee plant used in coffee production are Arabica and Robusta. Originally indigenous to the mountains of Yemen, Arabica accounts for roughly two thirds of the world's coffee production. It is also produced in the southwestern highlands of Ethiopia and southeastern Sudan, throughout Latin America, India and to some extent in Indonesia.

Arabica's preference for higher altitudes has earned it the name "mountain" coffee, such as the rare and expensive Jamaican Blue Mountain coffee.

Arabica beans produce a complex coffee taste of superior quality to the Robusta, which is why many coffee blends will boast their credentials as "100% Arabica".

Robusta, from the species *C. canephora*, accounts for roughly a third of the coffee produced worldwide. It is cheaper to grow since it thrives at lower altitudes. Robusta is produced in West and Central Africa, Brazil and South-East Asia, particularly Vietnam. It contains more than twice the caffeine content as Arabica beans, making it is more resistant to pests. Robusta tends to produce a brew that is more bitter than Arabica, and imparts an earthy, even musty taste.

However, before you decide to reject Robusta outright, you should know that only the lower grade Robusta winds up as freeze-dried instant coffee, whereas the premium Robusta crop is still used in espresso coffee blends. Coffee shops may use Arabica as their primary bean but, because it is more expensive to grow, a blend containing some Robusta makes the Arabica more affordable.

Many Italian purveyors use 10% Robusta in their blends for its capacity to improve the consistency of crema.

In France, where they enjoy its bitter taste, the ratio of Robusta to Arabica can be as high as 45:55.

It also comes down to personal taste. Most coffee drinkers are used to the taste of Robusta from the supermarket aisle. Therefore you may find you enjoy the bitter edge and body of the Robusta beans brings to the mellower taste of Arabica.

Coffee roasting

The roasting process forces moisture out of the bean and brings volatile oils to the surface of the bean. The essence of the espresso flavour is in these delicate oils. The darker the roast, the longer the bean has been roasted, and a dark roast can have less caffeine than a lighter roast. As the heat of the roaster forces moisture out of the bean, the bean expands but the weight, because of the extraction of moisture, diminishes.

There is no precise standardized terminology used to describe the coffee roast. Viennese, Italian, French and American are not the origin of the bean, but instead refer to the degree of roasting, and that depends on the standards of the roaster.

Finding the right blends

A good option for experimenting with the best espresso blend for you is to look at those offered by boutique coffee roasters. There are countless purveyors of fine coffee who select choice green beans, which they roast themselves and then combine into a range of different blends. Many of these roasters have an online presence where you can order excellent whole or ground coffee blends directly to your door. Some even offer sample packs for tasting to enable you to choose which blend suits you. Others even allow you to make your own blend of different regional coffees.

Coffee contains 800 different aromatic compounds – anything from hints of chocolate to smoky, cigar-like aftertones – and these boutique roasters have spent years perfecting different blends for a range of tastes, occasions and even health and ethical concerns.

- Fair Trade Certified

Much of the world's coffee crop is grown in developing countries. In recent years, it has become possible to support these producers better by purchasing fair trade certified coffee. This means that the coffee is bought directly from the farmers and growers at a fair price, rather than via conventional trade economics that discriminates against the poorest and weakest producers. A fair trade partnership helps to improve local sustainability and quality of life in these impoverished areas by channelling money into important community infrastructure such as schools and hospitals.

- Rainforest Alliance Certified

The Rainforest Alliance is an international non-profit group dedicated to the conservation of tropical forests that works to conserve biodiversity by transforming land-use and business practices to ensure sustainable livelihoods. Coffee that is Rainforest Alliance Certified (RFA) is derived from farms and forests where water, soil and wildlife habitat are conserved, where workers are treated well, and where families have access to education and health care. So both coffee consumers and the communities where coffee is produced benefit.

- Organic

For coffee to be certified organic, it means that no chemicals or were used to produce the coffee. It must be produced without artificial chemical substances including some pesticides and herbicides, and also with organic fertilizer.

- Decaffeinated

The "hit" that coffee-drinkers perceive they get from a sip of a good cup of coffee is often nothing to do with caffeine, but rather from the intense taste of the coffee.

Good decaffeinated coffee can still offer that hit but without the caffeine.

Decaffeination is usually carried out by the Swiss Water method pioneered by the Swiss Water Decaffeinated Coffee Company in the 1930s. Raw green coffee beans are soaked in hot water to release the caffeine and the beans discarded. The remaining water passes through a carbon filter that traps the caffeine but preserves the coffee solids. The resulting extract is used to capture caffeine from new green beans added to it, creating raw beans that are 99.9% caffeine free. The caffeine is lost but not the taste.

Those simply wanting to reduce their caffeine, not eliminate it entirely, might confine themselves to 100% Arabica beans only since these contain about half the caffeine as Robusta.

MACINAZIONE
– GRINDING THE BEANS

As anyone who has ever sniffed freshly ground coffee beans will know, the aroma and taste of the coffee is at its best immediately after the beans are ground.

In fact, the most discerning baristas will only grind beans for espresso directly before using them. Coffee puritans swear that it only takes 30 seconds in the open air for ground beans to become too stale for a good espresso. It is true that ground beans slowly lose their intensity over time, but this can be reduced if the coffee is properly stored.

How to store your coffee?

If you elect to purchase your coffee pre-ground, you need to remember that all coffee is highly perishable. This is especially true of ground coffee, since so much more surface area is exposed to the air. Because of this, coffee is often vacuum packed, although even this keeps the coffee fresh for only a few weeks. Be warned that many pre-packaged coffees imported into Australia are already some months old before they reach the supermarket shelves.

It is best, therefore, to grind your coffee beans yourself immediately prior to using or buy your coffee fresh each week. Or, if this is not practical, buy the smallest practical quantity you can manage, and store it in an airtight, moisture-proof container in a cool place.

A glass or ceramic container with a rubber seal is ideal.

Importantly, do NOT store coffee in the fridge or freezer. When cold coffee is brought out of your fridge into room temperature, a layer of water condenses on its surface which damages the aromatic oils of the coffee. Like tea, coffee attracts and absorbs foreign smells, so protect your coffee from contamination from other foodstuffs that may affect the taste.

Which grinder?

We all know there is no contest between ready-ground coffee and the coffee you grind yourself. Also, whole beans keep far longer than ground, so obtaining whole beans and grinding just before brewing is ideal. There are two main varieties of home coffee grinders – blade grinders and burr grinders.

- Blade grinders

These operate like a small home blender by using fast-moving blades to chop the beans. The grind produced by such machines varies from chunks to fine powder. This inconsistent grind is okay for stove-top or drip coffee makers, but not for pump- or piston-driven espresso machines that require a uniformly fine grind. Such grinders also heat the beans, which can tamper with the quality of the coffee.

- Burr grinders

Using a burr grinder will give homogeneous grinding so the particle size of the coffee is consistent and even, which is especially important for espresso. If the particle size of the coffee is uniform, equal amounts of the coffee's profile will be extracted. However, if the particle size of the coffee

varies, some particles will be over-extracted and some will be under-extracted, resulting in poor tasting coffee.

These grinders may be either electric or operated by hand. They contain corrugated steel burrs that rotate to shave the beans. The benefit of such machines is that may be adjusted to achieve different grinds, making them ideal for a range of different machines. They also minimise heat production that can affect the taste of the coffee.

Before investing in a home grinder, consider how much you wish to spend and how much time you are prepared to devote to use and maintenance. Manual burr grinders are cheaper but require some elbow grease to operate. The more expensive the electric machine, the greater degree of grind adjustment available, which is preferable. The correct grind is a vital step in preparing café-quality espresso – this may require a period of trial and error to fine-tune the consistency of the grind to your particular espresso machine. A grinder that does not achieve the exact grind you require for your coffee machine type will be a waste of money.

Some modern electric burr grinders include electronic sensors for precision grinding and a portion-control container that measures out the precise amount of coffee required each time. Certainly the cost of a burr grinder is worth the investment, because whole beans retain their freshness longer than pre-ground coffee, and you can adjust the grind to suit your machine to obtain that perfect cup of espresso coffee.

Like any equipment used to prepare food, grinders require maintenance and cleaning to be kept in optimal condition. There is little point grinding freshly roasted beans in a machine that contains old coffee residue that has turned rancid.

Which grind?

Whether grinding your coffee yourself or buying it pre-ground, ensure the grind is appropriate for your machine:

PLUNGER : Medium Fine
FILTER/DRIP METHOD : Fine
ESPRESSO AND STOVETOP : Very Fine
GREEK AND TURKISH : Powder

The grind determines how fast the coffee is extracted. Too coarse a grind will produce watery coffee with no crema. Too fine a grind will over-extract the coffee and make it bitter.

Also, the grind has to be uniform in order to ensure the best taste. Generally speaking, the faster the brewing method, the finer the grind required.

For your espresso machine, the beans must be ground fine, but not too fine. If the grind is too fine – a powder grind – water cannot flow through the grind even under pressure. A powder grind feels like flour when rubbed between the fingers. A fine grind should feel gritty, like salt.

If the water flows too slowly or not at all, the grind is too fine for your machine. Another variable is the quality of the coffee used and the pressure applied when tamping the coffee in the coffee basket.

A more powerful machine develops greater pressure and therefore takes a finer grind. However, if the grind is too fine, or the coffee tamped too compactly, the water under pressure in the brew head will not be able to flow through the grind and coffee may spurt from around the filter holder.

The proper grind for your particular machine is critical to extracting a crema espresso. You will need to test the fineness of the grind at different indexes on the grinder before determining the optimum grind for your machine.

If you are desperate, you can pound the roasted beans using a mortar and pestle, but this generally reduces the bean to the power consistency required for Greek or Turkish coffee and is too fine for espresso.

Macchina
– THE ESPRESSO MACHINE

Electric, non-pump machines are the highest selling coffee machines for the home market today. These entry-level machines are cheaper than their pump counterparts, but will still produce a serviceable long black. However, non-pump machines rely on steam pressure and so do not provide enough force for creating café-quality crema, which is the basis for many coffee beverage as well as the prerequisite for producing coffee art in the home.

To bring the café experience into your kitchen, what you need is a piston-lever or pump-driven machine that generates sufficient pump pressure to force hot water through the fine coffee grind.

Espresso machine pressure is measured in atmospheres (ATM) or pounds per square inch (psi). Non-pump machines only generate pressure to an average of 3 ATM or 44 psi. Pump-driven machine, on the other hand, achieve pressures of up to 9–17 ATM or 135–250 psi.

The latest technology in the home espresso machine is the thermoblock system, which replaces the boiler with a thermal block. Because the water is flash-heated by the thermoblock, steam is continuously available for frothing or steaming milk (while there is still water in the reservoir).

If you are wanting to improve your skills as a barista and experiment with coffee art, you require at least a pump-driven or piston-lever machine. However, if ease of operation is more important, there are also automatic machines that complete the whole ritual of coffee making for you, with programs for different coffee types at the click of a button. Espresso machines are also available in combination with ordinary drip model for households who require espresso-drinkers and drip-coffee drinkers to be catered for by a single unit.

MANO
– THE SKILLS OF THE BARISTA

As "mano" is the Italian word for hand, this final M refers to the talents of the barista. "Barista" is the Italian word for bartender, although it has come to refer specifically to a person skilled in the art of coffee making.

Even if you have purchased a state-of-the-art espresso machine, making coffee still requires practice. The most important thing is to know your equipment, including the grinder and the espresso machine. Be sure to read the manual that comes with the machine. Thankfully, home espresso machines today require less skill, but the espresso maker is still a sophisticated piece of equipment that requires some initial self-training to use. For example, you need to know how to fill your filter basket properly, how to tamp the ground coffee, the best movements required for frothing the milk.

Like all skills, making the perfect espresso requires practice. There is no rewind switch or undo button when making a cup of coffee, so achieving the perfect crema beings with some trial and error. But, don't take it too seriously – learning to become a home barista is part of the fun of owning your machine. With patience, you will eventually learn to pull every shot with the beautiful crema that is the mark of true espresso.

To make great coffee in your coffee machine, always follow the 5 basic steps...

- Empty old coffee grounds thoroughly
- Rinse out old grounds
- Wipe the handle
- Pack the coffee gently
- Tamp with reasonable pressure (not too hard)

COFFEE ART

If making coffee is a science – from the roasting and grinding of the beans to the perfect brewing temperature to extract the ultimate coffee – then creating unique images on the coffee surface is the art.

Coffee art or latte art requires a perfect combination of crema and steamed milk foam. The milk is steamed using the wand on the espresso machine until the stainless steel jug feels too hot to touch for longer than a second but not boiling. The resulting froth – sometimes called microfoam – has a smooth, meringue-like texture, unlike the big-bubbled macrofoam that is no good for making coffee art.

The secret to creating the coffee art canvas is the pour. The milk should be poured at a consistent rate into the centre of the espresso so that the milk disappears under the brown layer of crema or is layered on, depending which design you wish to achieve. A teaspoon and other tools are used add final droplets of milk foam, which are then manipulated against the brown base to create interesting designs. You will be amazed at the dizzying array of patterns you can create with a skewer or a teaspoon: from seagulls to hearts to flowers to leaves to lips to smiley faces!

Coffee Art

A lot of care needs to be taken when
pouring the milk so you don't destroy
the crema. Spoons, toothpicks and other
pointed utensils may be used together
with a good pouring jug to place the froth
on the coffee and create a desired shape.
Coffee art is only limited by the barista's
artistry, skills and imagination.

Free-Poured Patterns

The hardest form of coffee art is "free pouring". This is where we get into creating art, such as the heart, rosetta, tulip and other designs.

These are created by simply moving the milk jug a certain way when pouring. Don't be disappointed if you can't get these patterns correct immediately as they are hard to do and require a lot of practice. Ultimately you will need to ensure that you are getting perfect shots and perfect milk every time in order to start trying these designs.

POURING THE MILK

You should texture the milk whilst the espresso is being brewed.

Start with the tip of your jug on the edge of the cup and pour steadily. Once the cup is about half full, lower the pour close to the crema and the foam should appear.

You should pour the milk as soon as possible. Hold the cup on its ear and slightly at an angle. Start pouring the milk slowly into the crema. You do not want to pour too slowly, this will leave the foam behind in the jug. You also do not want to pour too quick because this will break the crema apart. Pour slowly in a few spots in the cup to break through the crema.

Start pouring the milk into the back of the cup once the cup seems just more than half full. Now slowly but very steadily move the pitcher from side to side. This is a wrist movement and should be done just slightly. The milk should not swing from side to side in the jug. Keep moving it side to side in one spot in the cup until you see the foam appearing. If you see distinct white lines forming, you're on the right track. Keep practising and eventually you will be rewarded with your own latte design.

Once you see the foam break through the crema you can start pouring patterns.

Heart

1   Pour slowly in the middle to settle the crema so you can have a base to work with.

2   About halfway through, start tilting the jug forward to release some froth.

3   Continue pouring into the middle and let the white circle form.

4   Near the top of the cup start tilting the jug back upwards and move to the other side of the cup in a scooping motion.

Tulip

1   This one is a lot like the heart but you start and stop to get different layers to create the Tulip.

2   Start pouring at one end of the cup and once you get your first blob of froth in the coffee, stop.

3   Move the jug closer to you and start pouring again until you have a smaller blob.

4   Near the top of the cup start tilting the jug back upwards and move to the other side of the cup in a scooping motion.

Rosetta

1   To start with, pour slowly to settle the crema to give you
    a good base to start. This allows the milk to separate to
    form the pattern.

2   About halfway through pouring, move the jug from side
    to side until you see the foam appearing on the surface.
    Keep moving the jug from side to side until you see
    curved white lines appear. Now slowly move the jug
    backwards while still moving it from side to side.

3   Once you have reached the edge of the cup, start tilting
    the jug back upwards and move back down the centre of
    the leaves in a scooping motion.

Note Quick movements from side to side will create a rosetta with
lots of leaves. Slow movements from side to side will create fewer
and thicker leaves.

Double Rosetta

1   To start with, pour slowly to settle the crema to give you a good base to start. This allows the milk to separate to form the pattern.

2   About halfway through pouring, move the jug from side to side until you see the foam appearing on the surface. Keep moving the jug from side to side until you see curved white lines appear. Now slowly move the jug along one side of the cup while still moving it from side to side.

3   Once you have reached the edge of the cup, start tilting the jug back upwards and move it back down the centre of the leaves in a scooping motion.

4   Repeat steps 2–4 on the other side of the cup to achieve your other rosetta.

Note Quick movements from side to side will create a rosetta with lots of leaves. Slow movements from side to side will create fewer and thicker leaves.

Rosetta with Chocolate Wreaths

1   To start with, pour slowly to settle the crema to give you a good base to start. This allows the milk to separate to form the pattern.

2   About halfway through pouring, move the jug from side to side until you see the foam appearing on the surface. Keep moving the jug from side to side until you see curved white lines appear. Now slowly move the jug backwards while still moving it from side to side.

3   Once you have reached the edge of the cup, start tilting the jug back upwards and move back down the centre of the leaves in a scooping motion.

4   Using your chocolate sauce bottle, draw two zigzags of chocolate either side of the rosetta. Using a clean skewer starting at top of cup, dip in and drag down through the middle of the chocolate zigzags to create your wreaths.

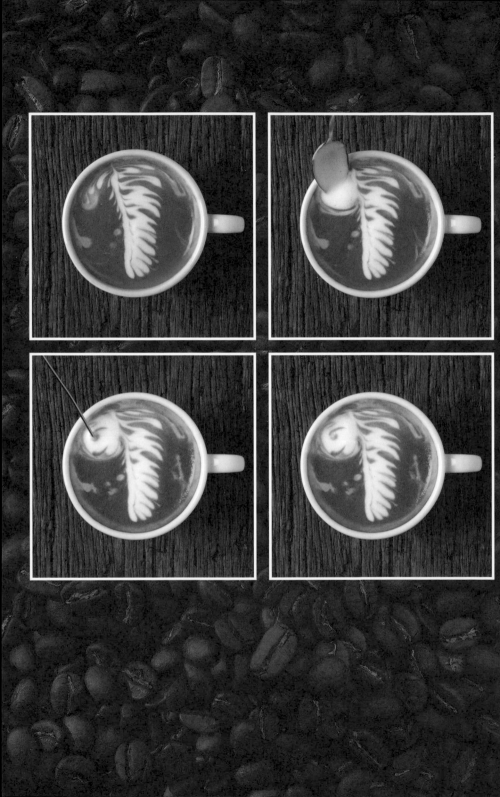

Indian Head

1   Pour a rosetta (see page 41).

2   Use a teaspoon to scoop out some froth and place on left-hand side of rosetta.

3   Using a clean skewer, dip into the crema and etch an eye and a mouth.

Heart with Chain of Hearts

1   Pour a heart (see page 37) on one side of the cup.

2   Using a spoon, scoop out some white froth from your jug
    and place a white dot on the brown base on the other
    side of the big heart. Repeat this two more times below
    the first white dot.

3   Using a clean skewer starting at the top white dot, dip
    your skewer into the crema and drag through the centre
    of all the white dots.

Etched Patterns

Milk etching is a form of coffee art that is done by using the milk froth to create a contrast on the coffee.

A lot of care should be taken when pouring the milk so as not to destroy the crema. Spoons, toothpicks, the tip of the thermometer or similar utensils may be used to place the froth on the coffee and create the desired pattern. This may take a little more time but always remember it is more important to serve a good tasting hot coffee, so don't try anything too fancy too fast.

Seashell

1   Pour into centre of espresso to achieve a white circle on top of coffee. If in your pour you don't achieve a white circle in the middle of the crema, use a spoon to scoop some froth out of the jug and place in the middle of the cup.

2   Dip the handle of a spoon or a skewer into the white circle.

3   Pretend your cup is a clock face. At 12 o'clock at the edge of the cup, dip your skewer or spoon handle into the coffee and drag back to the middle. Repeat this several times, making your way around the cup.

4   Using a clean skewer, start in the middle and draw a swirl from the centre to the edge of the cup.

Flower

1 Pour into centre of espresso to achieve a white circle on top of coffee.

2 Using a skewer, dip into the white circle, then dip your painted skewer into the crema and drag back to the middle using an arc motion.

3 Repeat this several times, making your way around the cup.

Pinwheel

1   To start with, pour slowly to settle the crema to give you
a good base to start. This allows the milk to separate to
form the pattern.

2   About halfway through pouring, tilt the jug closer to
the coffee angled more open so the froth can start
separating, leaving you with a white blob on top of
the coffee.

3   Using a skewer, dip into the white circle, then dip
your painted skewer into the crema and drag back to
the middle using an arc motion. The more lines the
better definition.

4   Once finished etching the lines, use a clean skewer to
dip into some brown crema then dip skewer into line tips
around edge of cup. Continue until all lines have a dot at
the end.

Sun

1 Pour into centre of **espresso** to achieve a white circle on top of coffee. If in your pour you don't achieve a white circle in the middle of the crema, use a spoon to scoop some froth out of the jug and place in the middle of the cup.

2 Using a skewer, dip the tip into the white edge of the circle and make your way around the whole circle using an "S" motion.

3 Using a clean skewer, dip into the crema and draw a face in the centre of the white circle.

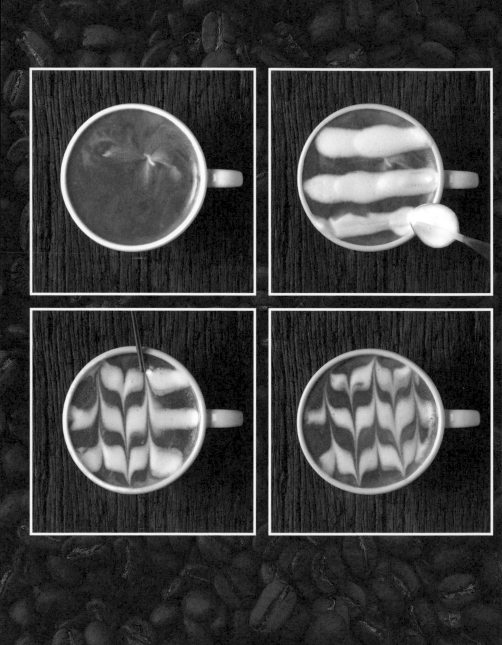

Seagulls

1   Pour your coffee gently to create a brown base on top.

2   Use a spoon to scoop some froth milked out of your jug and create some parallel lines.

3   Place a skewer at the top of the parallel lines. Drag the skewer through the lines, move it to the side and drag in the opposite direction similar to the spacing shown. Continue until the cup is full of seagulls.

Chain of Hearts

1 Slowly pour your coffee to get a nice brown base.

2 Using a spoon, scoop out some white froth from your jug and place a white dot on the brown base. Repeat this two more times below the first white dot.

3 Using a clean skewer starting at the top white dot, dip your skewer into the crema and drag through the centre of all the white dots.

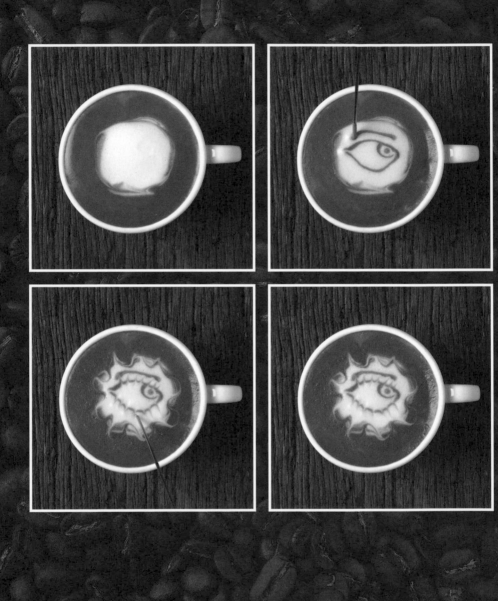

Egyptian Eye

1   Pour into centre of espresso to achieve a white circle on
    top of coffee. If in your pour you don't achieve a white
    circle in the middle of the crema, use a spoon to scoop
    some froth out of the jug and place in the middle of
    the cup.

2   Using your skewer, dip deeply into the crema and etch an
    oval into the white circle. Dip again and draw an eyebrow
    above the oval. Clean skewer, dip again into crema and
    draw a circle inside the oval on the right-hand side.
    Dip into crema again and draw a pupil inside of the circle.

3   Using a clean skewer dip into the oval and drag out to
    create the eye lashes.

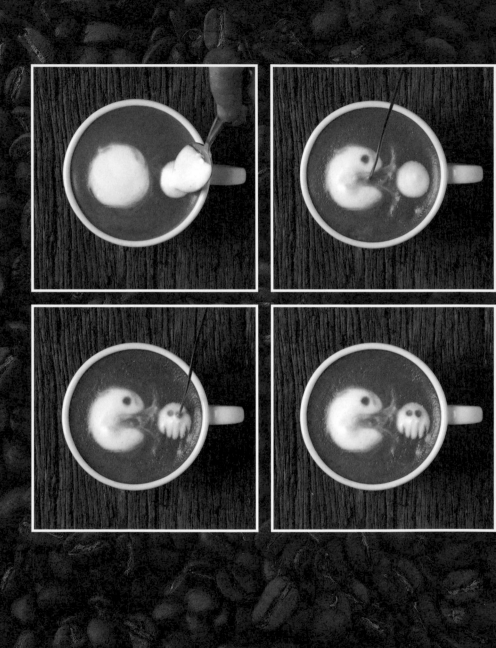

Pac Man Eating a Ghost

1   Pour your coffee trying to achieve a white circle on the left-hand side of the cup. Once again, if you don't achieve the white circle use a teaspoon to scoop out some froth and place on left-hand side of the coffee cup.

2   Use a teaspoon to scoop out some froth and place smaller circle next to the big white circle.

3   Using a clean skewer, start outside the big circle and drag into the middle creating a wide mouth. Using a clean skewer, dip into crema and give the pac man an eye.

4   Using a clean skewer on the bottom of the smaller white circles, drag your skewer up a couple of times to create a ghost tail. Clean skewer off, dip into crema and etch some eyes on the ghost.

Monkey

1 Pour coffee slowly to achieve a nice brown base.

2 Use a desert spoon to scoop out some froth from the jug and place a big big white circle at bottom of cup. Use a teaspoon to scoop out some froth and place a smaller white circle on top of the larger circle. Use your teaspoon again for the two white blobs for the ears.

3 Using a clean skewer, dip deeply into crema and etch the line for mouth with teeth in the big white blob. Clean skewer off, dip again in crema and etch nostrils. Clean skewer again and etch eyes in top white blob.

Panda

1   Pour coffee slowly to achieve a nice brown base.

2   Use a desert spoon to scoop out some froth from the jug and place a big white circle in centre of cup. Use a teaspoon to scoop out some white froth from your jug and place the ears on the edge of the big white blob.

3   Clean teaspoon off, scoop out some crema and place the eyes and the inner ears.

4   Clean teaspoon off, scoop out some white froth from jug again and place on top of brown eyes.

5   Using a clean skewer, dip into the crema then dip into the eyes and etch mouth.

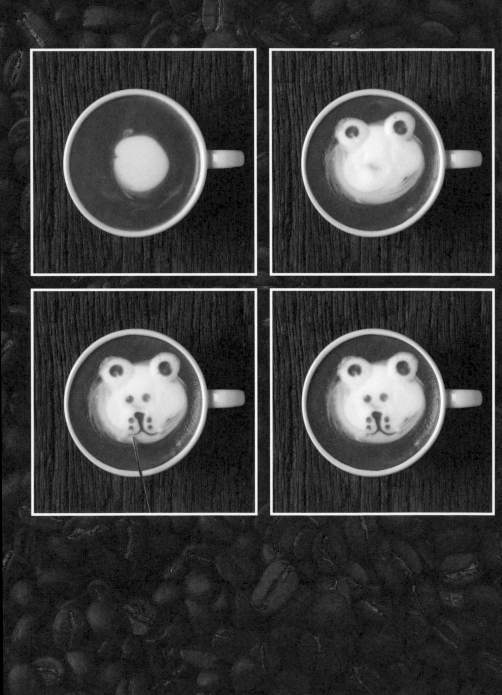

Bear Face

1. Pour into centre of espresso to achieve a white circle on top of coffee. If in your pour you don't achieve a white circle in the middle of the crema, use a spoon to scoop some froth out of the jug and place in the middle of the cup.

2. Use a teaspoon to scoop out some froth and place the ears on top the white circle.

3. Using a skewer, dip into the crema and dip into the white ears to create a contrast.

4. Dip again into the crema and etch some eyes and a mouth.

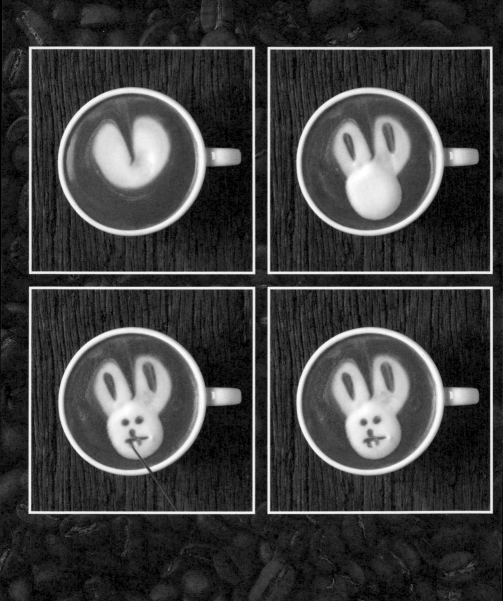

Bunny

1 Pour a heart (see page 37).

2 Use a dessert spoon to scoop out some froth from the jug and place below heart.

3 Using a clean skewer, dip into the crema and draw ears, nose, mouth and teeth.

4 Dip your skewer again and etch some eyes.

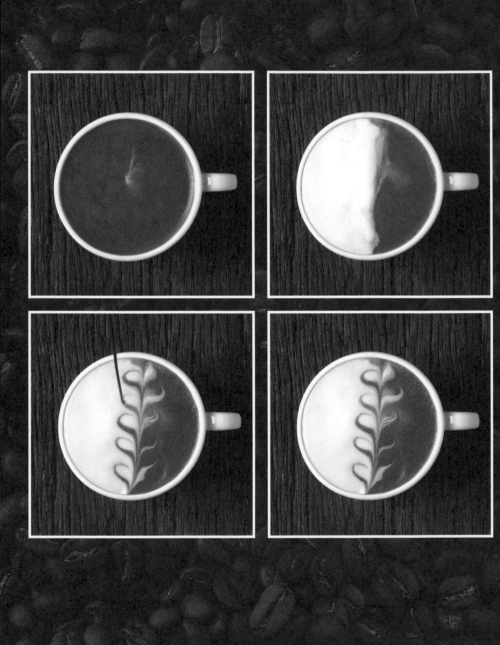

Shoelace

1   Slowly pour your coffee to get a nice brown base.

2   Use a spoon to scoop out froth from your milk jug and cover half the coffee with it, ensuring you keep an even line in the middle.

3   Using a clean skewer, dip into the white side and drag it into the brown crema. Whilst dragging upwards move your skewer left and right.

4   Once at the top, drag your skewer down the middle to the bottom of the cup.

Orchid Flower

1   Pour into centre of espresso to achieve a white circle on top of coffee. If in your pour you don't achieve a white circle in the middle of the crema, use a spoon to scoop some froth out of the jug and place in the middle of the cup.

2   Using a thermometer or thick skewer, dip into the white circle then dip into the brown crema at 12 o'clock on the rim of the cup and drag back to the centre. Repeat this at 3 o'clock, 6 o'clock and 9 o'clock.

3   Using a skewer, dip into the centre of the white circle and drag out through the middle of each petal.

4   Dip the skewer into the crema and place a brown dot in the centre of the flower.

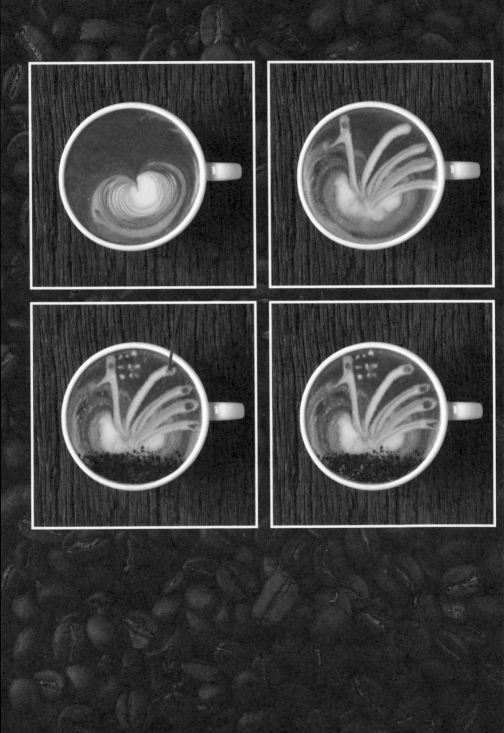

Peacock

1 Pour your coffee to leave yourself with a thick white line. You can always cheat and use a spoon to draw the white line. Use your spoon to create a head on top of the thick white line.

2 Using the handle of the spoon, dip into the white froth and etch a white line in the brown crema dragging back to the white line to create one of the feathers. Repeat this process four times.

3 Using a clean skewer, etch a mouth and an eye.

4 Using a clean skewer, dip into the white froth and then dip into the brown crema above the head to make some white dots – these are the peacock's head feathers.

5 Using a clean skewer, dip into some brown crema then mark the end of each feather. Use a chocolate powder shaker, dust chocolate over the bottom of the pattern.

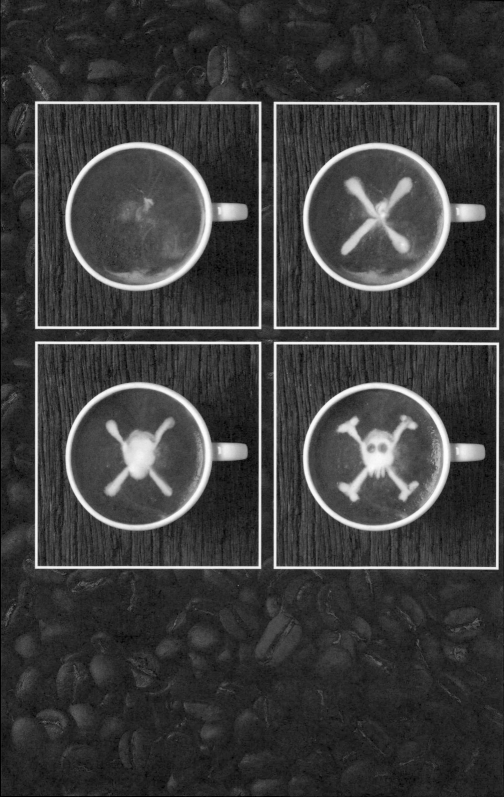

Skull and Crossbones

1 Slowly pour your coffee to get a nice brown base.

2 Dip the handle of the spoon into the white froth and etch the bones by dragging back to the centre.

3 Using a clean skewer at the edge of the bones, dip into the crema to make the joints on the bones.

4 Using a clean skewer starting at bottom of the circle, dip into the crema and drag up to create teeth for the skull.

5 Dip skewer into crema and etch some eyes.

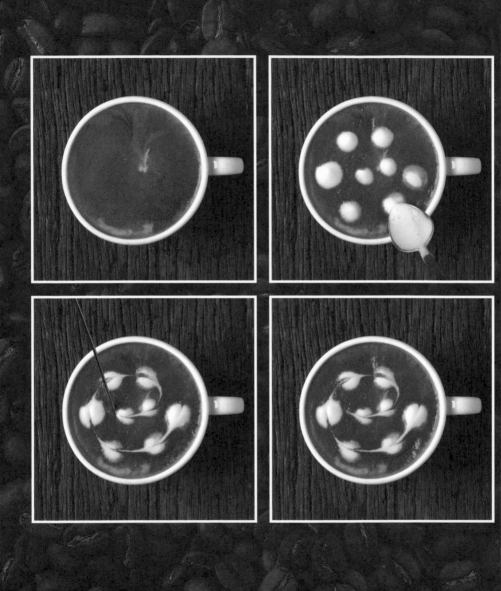

Swirl Chain of Hearts

1 Slowly pour your coffee to get a nice brown base.

2 Using a spoon, scoop out some white froth from your jug and place a white dot near the centre of the coffee. Repeat this step in a swirl motion until your reach the rim of the cup.

3 Using a clean skewer, start at the white dot nearest the rim of the cup, dip your skewer into the crema and drag through the centre of all the white dots, making your way to the middle.

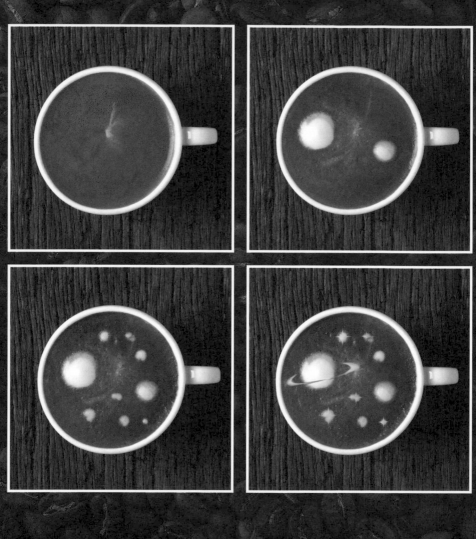

Galaxy

1 Pour your coffee gently to achieve a nice brown base.

2 Using a spoon, scoop out some froth and place two circles in the coffee.

3 Using a skewer, dip into the white froth and place some random white dots in the coffee.

4 Using a clean skewer, dip in the biggest circle and drag out and then back through the circle, finishing on other side.

5 Using a clean skewer, dip into the centre of the small white dots and drag out into the crema to make the star.

Patterns with Chocolate

The easiest way to make coffee art is to use chocolate syrup to form the design. This is because the finished product is not dependent on the way the coffee is poured. However, it is always good practice to keep as much of the crema on the coffee as possible.

You should never use chocolate milkshake topping for chocolate etching as it destroys the taste and quality of the finished coffee. The best option is to use a good brand of chocolate powder and mix it with boiling water to form a chocolate paste that sits well on the coffee. Make sure the powder is well mixed and there are no clumps of chocolate powder as a clump may block up the sauce bottle. An even better option is to use espresso shots to mix the chocolate instead of the boiling water – you will find that the resulting effect is far superior.

Bottles suitable for this application are readily available at your local craft shop or discount variety store.

Note that chocolate etching should only be placed on cappuccinos, hot chocolates and mochas.

CHOCOLATE SAUCE RECIPE

To create your chocolate sauce for your coffees, extract a 30 ml (1 fl oz) espresso shot, add 6 dessert spoons of chocolate powder and mix thoroughly. Your sauce should be nice and thick and easy to work with. If it's too thin and watery, add more chocolate powder. If too thick, add another 30 ml (1 fl oz) shot of espresso.

Chocolate Flower

1 Using a craft bottle filled with chocolate sauce, draw
   a circle in the centre of the cup. Repeat this process,
   drawing a circle around the previous one.

2 Pretend your cup is a clock-face. At 12 o'clock at the
   edge of the cup, dip your skewer or spoon handle into the
   coffee and drag back to the middle. Repeat this process
   at 3 o'clock, 6 o'clock and 9 o'clock. Make sure you wipe
   the chocolate off your skewer each time.

3 Using a clean skewer, dip in the middle and drag out to
   the edge of the cup to create petals.

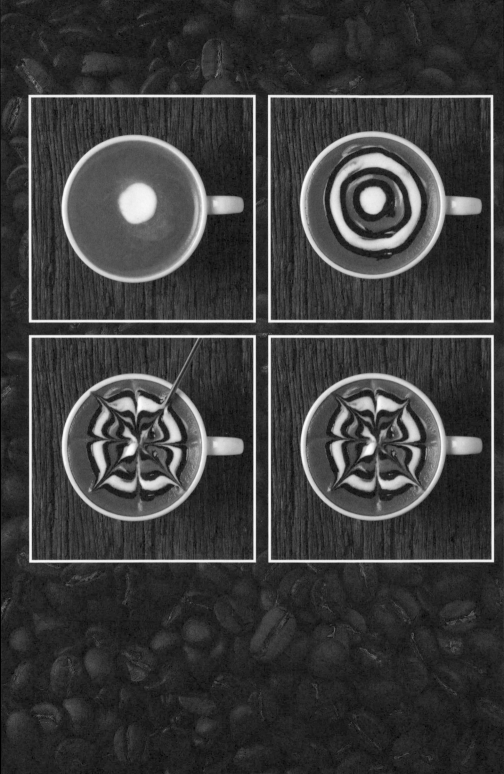

Morning Star

1   Pour into centre of espresso to achieve a white circle on top of coffee.

2   Using a chocolate sauce bottle, draw a circle around the white blob. Then draw another bigger chocolate circle around the smaller one.

3   Using a skewer, dip into crema outside the biggest chocolate circle and pull directly into the centre of the circle and lift out gently. Repeat this three or more times around the white circle.

4   Place a clean skewer deep into the centre and drag out to the edge of the cup midway between two of the existing lines. Repeat three more times around the circle.

Flower with Choc Outline

1 Pour into centre of espresso to achieve a white circle on top of coffee.

2 Using a chocolate sauce bottle, draw a circle around the white blob. Then draw another bigger chocolate circle around the smaller one.

3 Using a skewer, dip into crema outside the biggest chocolate circle and pull directly into the centre of the circle and lift out gently.

4 Once you have several petals, place a clean skewer deep into the centre of the petals and drag out to the edge of the cup. Repeat with each petal.

Butterfly

1   Pour a heart (see page 37).

2   Using a chocolate sauce bottle, trace the outline of
the heart.

3   Using a clean skewer, dip into white froth and etch some
antennas at the top of the heart.

4   Using a clean skewer, dip into the crema on one side of
heart and drag into the middle. Repeat on other side.

5   Using a clean skewer, dip into crema at bottom of heart
and drag up to give you the butterfly body.

6   Using a clean skewer, dip into right top wing and drag
out towards the rim of the cup. Repeat on left top wing.

7   Using a clean skewer, dip into the bottom right wing and
drag out to the rim of the cup. Repeat on left bottom wing.
Finally add four dots of chocolate sauce.

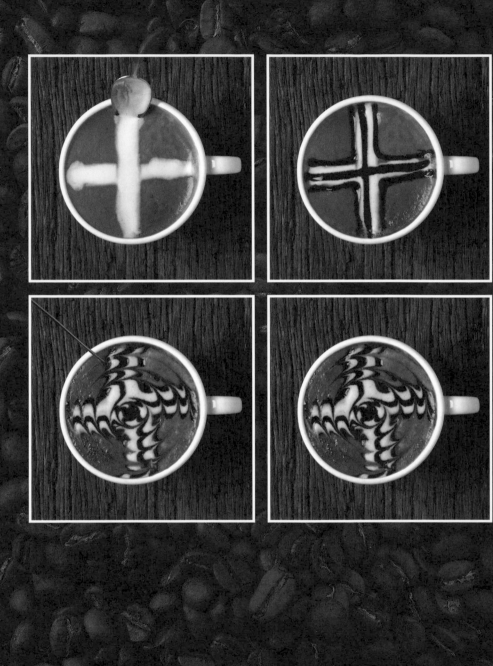

Choc Swirls

1   Pour coffee slowly to achieve a nice brown base.

2   Use a spoon to scoop out some froth from the jug and put a line of white across the middle of the coffee. Repeat again, creating a white cross in your coffee.

3   Using your chocolate sauce bottle, follow the outside outline of the white cross. Then place another chocolate cross in the middle of the white cross.

4   Using a clean skewer, dip it deep in the middle of the coffee and start swirling outwards until you reach the rim of the cup.

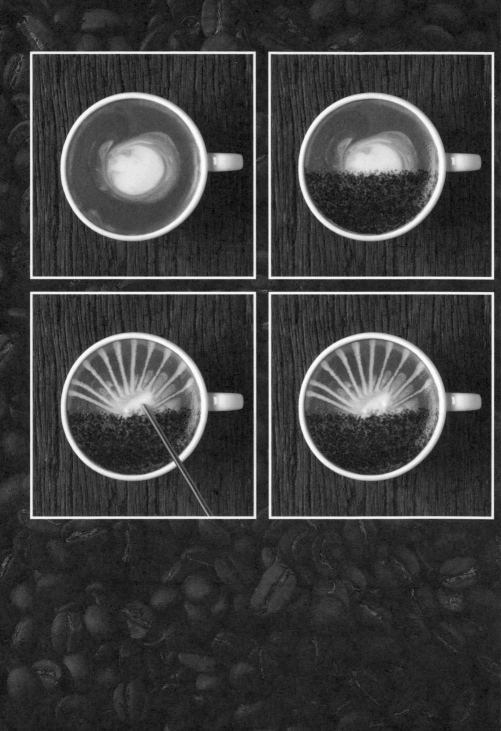

Sunrise

1   Slowly pour your coffee to get a nice brown base.

2   Using a dessert spoon scoop out some froth from the jug
    and place in the middle of the coffee. Use a chocolate
    powder shaker, dust chocolate on half of the coffee,
    covering half the white circle.

3   Using a clean skewer, dip into the white semi-circle,
    then pull out and dip in at far left of the cup rim and
    drag back to the white circle, creating a ray of sunshine.
    Repeat several times, making your way right.

Spiderweb

1　Slowly pour your coffee to get a nice brown base.

2　Using a chocolate bottle, start squeezing chocolate sauce into the middle of the coffee. Make a circular motion with your hand, getting bigger and bigger until you get to the the edge of the cup.

3　Using a clean skewer, start at the edge of the cup and drag it into the middle. Repeat this process several times, making your way around the cup. Remember to clean your skewer each time for a nice clean finish.

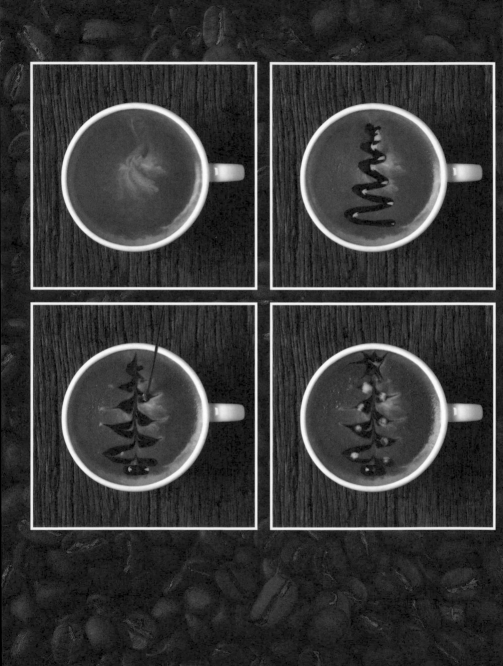

Christmas Tree

1   Pour your coffee gently to achieve a nice brown base.

2   Using a chocolate sauce bottle, start at bottom of the cup
    and draw a zig zag, starting big at the bottom but getting
    smaller as you make your way to the top.

3   Using a clean skewer, dip into the crema at the bottom
    of the Christmas tree and drag to the top. As a result you
    will be left with leaves on each side. Using clean skewer,
    dip in the centre of each leaf and drag out.

4   Using a chocolate sauce bottle, draw a small circle on
    top the tree. Using a clean skewer, dip into the centre
    of the circle and drag out. Repeat a couple of times so it
    resembles a star.

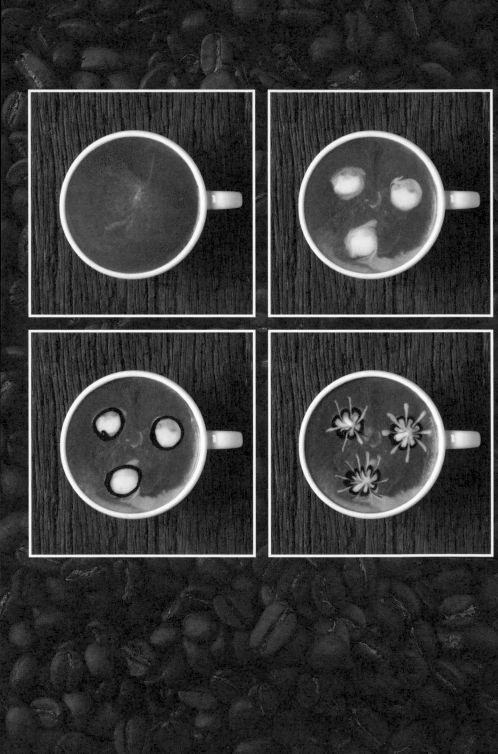

Lily Ponds

1 Slowly pour your coffee to get a nice brown base.

2 Using a spoon, scoop out some white froth and place 3 circles on the brown base.

3 Using a chocolate sauce bottle, put a chocolate ring around each of the white circles.

4 Using a clean skewer, dip into the white, then pull out and place outside of chocolate ring and drag back to middle.

5 Repeat this till you have several white lines around each lily.

Boat

1 Pour into centre of espresso to achieve a white circle on top of coffee. If in your pour you don't achieve a white circle in the middle of the crema, use a spoon to scoop some froth out of the jug and place in the middle of the cup.

2 Using a chocolate shaker, dust half the coffee.

3 Using a chocolate sauce bottle, follow the outline of the white semi-circle. Next, draw a thick line above the choc powder, then draw a mast and sail.

4 Using a clean skewer, dip into the white circle below the chocolate outline and drag out to the rim of the cup. Repeat this several times moving from left to right. Make sure you wipe your skewer clean each time to ensure a nice clean finish.

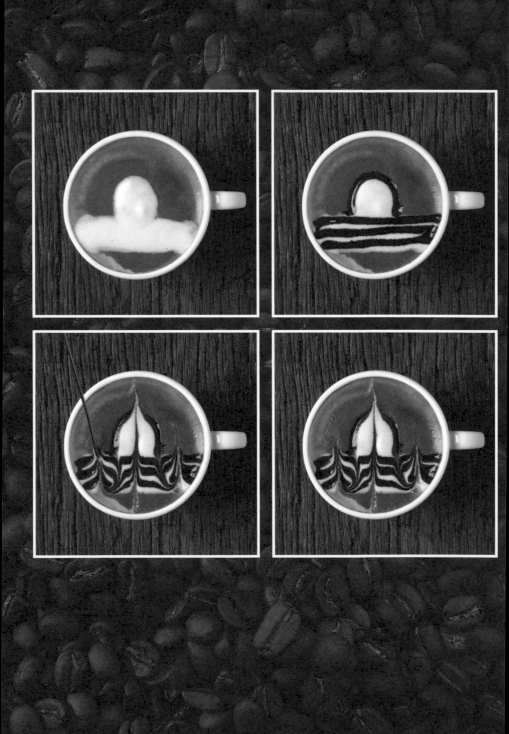

Taj Mahal

1   Pour coffee slowly to achieve a nice brown base. Using a spoon, scoop out some froth from the jug and place a white line across your coffee below the centre. Scoop out some more white froth and place a white circle in the middle and on top of the white line.

2   Using a chocolate sauce bottle, draw three parallel lines across your white line and outline the white circle with chocolate sauce.

3   Using a clean skewer, dip into the crema below the chocolate lines and drag up through the centre of the white circle.

4   Using a clean skewer, dip into where the chocolate circle starts, drag down through the parallel lines and do a u-shape motion dragging back up through the parallel line again and up to the top rim of the cup. Repeat this process on the other side of the coffee.

Coffee with Text

1   Pour your coffee gently to achieve a nice brown base.

2   Use a chocolate shaker and dust half your coffee
    with chocolate.

3   Using a chocolate sauce bottle, draw a name or
    statement in the coffee.

Note I use this when I sometimes make a mistake and write "sorry"
on top of the coffee – customers love it!

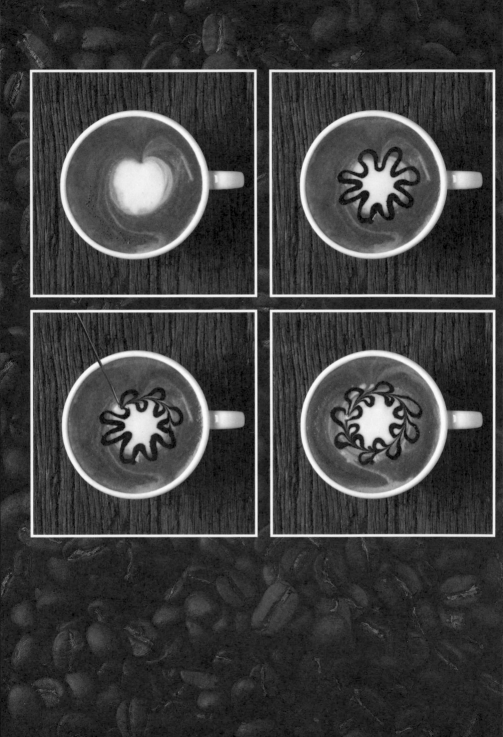

Crown

1 Pour into centre of espresso to achieve a white circle on top of coffee. If in your pour you don't achieve a white circle in the middle of the crema, use a spoon to scoop some froth out of the jug and place in the middle of the cup.

2 Using a chocolate sauce bottle, draw your crown around the white circle.

3 Using a skewer, dip in at the edge of the white circle and drag around the edge of the white circle to give your crown a clean finish.

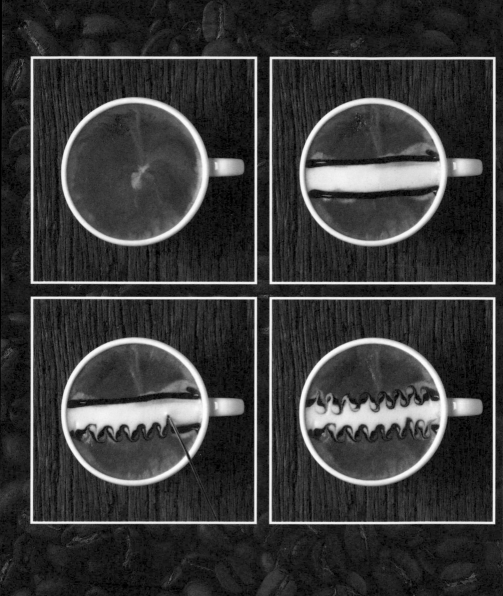

Caterpillar

1 Pour your coffee slowly to achieve a brown base.

2 Using a spoon a scoop out some froth from the jug and place a white line across the cup.

3 Draw a chocolate line along each edge of your white line.

4 Using a skewer, dip in at the start of the chocolate line and drag it back and forth from the white line and brown base, following the chocolate line. Repeat with other chocolate line.

Choc Sun

1 Pour your coffee slowly to achieve a nice brown base.

2 Using a chocolate sauce bottle, draw a circle in the centre. Draw another circle around the smaller one, then a third circle outside the second.

3 Using a skewer starting on the outside of the circles, dip into the crema and drag into the centre. Wipe your skewer each time. Repeat this process several times, making your way around the circle.

4 Using a clean skewer, drag out from the centre between each of the existing lines, using a curving motion.

Quick and Simple

1   Pour coffee and use a spoon to cover it with white froth.

2   Using a chocolate sauce bottle, draw a random
    continuous circle on the white base. The more circles,
    the more effective the design.

3   Using a skewer starting on the outside of the circles,
    dip into the coffee and drag into the centre. Wipe your
    skewer each time. Repeat this process several times,
    making your way around the circle.

Note You can use a brown base also but white gives
more definition.

Coffee Varieties

Many people drink coffee in its well-known variations, such as cappuccino, caffè latte, flat white, espresso, macchiato and long black. However, there are many other specialty coffees available and we have listed a number of these in this chapter. Drink on and enjoy the wonderful tastes of beautifully brewed coffee.

Shot Variables

The main variables in a shot of espresso are the size and length. Terminology is standard, but precise sizes and proportions vary substantially. Cafés generally have a standard shot (size and length), such as "triple ristretto", only varying the number of shots in espresso-based drinks such as lattes, but not changing the extraction – changing between a double and a triple require changing the filter basket size, while changing between ristretto, normale, and lungo require changing the grind.

Size

The size can be a single, double, or triple, which correspond roughly to a 30, 60 or 90 ml (1, 2 or 3 fl oz) standard (normale) shot, and use a proportional amount of ground coffee, roughly 8, 15, and 21 grams (¼, ½ and ⅔ oz); correspondingly sized filter baskets are used. The single shot is the traditional shot size, being the maximum that could easily be pulled on a lever machine, while the double is the standard shot today.

Single baskets are sharply tapered or stepped down in diameter to provide comparable depth to the double baskets and, therefore, comparable resistance to water pressure.

In espresso-based drinks, particularly larger milk-based drinks, a drink with three or four shots of espresso will be called a "triple" or "quad", respectively, but this does not mean that the shots themselves are triple or quadruple shots.

Length

The length of the shot can be ristretto (restricted), normale/ standard (normal), or lungo (long): these correspond to a smaller or larger drink with the same amount of ground coffee and same level of extraction. Proportions vary, and the volume (and low density) of crema make volume-based comparisons difficult (precise measurement uses the mass of the drink), but proportions of 1:1, 1:2, and 1:3–4 are common for ristretto, normale, and lungo, corresponding to 30, 60 and 90–120 ml (1, 2, and 3-4 fl oz) for a double shot. Ristretto is the most commonly used of these terms, and double or triple ristrettos are particularly associated with artisanal espresso.

Ristretto, normale, and lungo are not simply the same shot, stopped at different times – this will result in an underextracted shot (if run too short a time) or an overextracted shot (if run too long a time). Rather, the grind is adjusted (finer for ristretto, coarser for lungo) so that the target volume is achieved by the time extraction finishes.

Espresso (Short Black)

Espresso is an Italian name for a coffee beverage. In Italy, the rise of espresso consumption coincided with the growth of urban populations. Espresso bars provided a place to meet, and coffee prices were controlled by local authorities provided the coffee was consumed standing up. This encouraged the "stand at the bar" culture.

A true Italian espresso is 30 ml (1 fl oz) of beverage with a thick, golden brown crema on the surface. True espresso is a complex beverage, combining a special blend of Arabica beans, darkly roasted, finely ground, densely packed and quickly brewed under pressure in individual servings. Properly brewed espresso with crema has a uniquely smooth and creamy bittersweet taste that captures the full essence of the beans, a distinctive taste not found in any other type of coffee.

ESPRESSO (SHORT BLACK)

---

1 Firmly tamp ground coffee to ensure that the water flow is restricted.
2 The pour/extraction should take approximately 30 seconds.
3 Serve in a small 90 ml (3 fl oz) ceramic glass or demitasse cup with a layer of golden crema on top.

Note The size of an espresso can be a single or "solo" (30 ml/1 fl oz), double or "doppio" (60 ml/2 f loz), or triple or "triplo" (90 ml/3 fl oz). The length of the shot can also be varied – ristretto (restricted), normale (normal) or lungo (long).

Long Black

160 ml (5 ⅓ fl oz) cup
⅗ hot water
⅖ espresso (2 shots)

Long black is made by laying a double shot of espresso over hot water (not boiling) – the hot water also comes from the espresso machine.

The order in which a long black is made is important, as reversing it (e.g. espresso first, water second) will destroy the crema from the espresso shots. The espresso should be full bodied, with a good crema.

LONG BLACK

1 Place 90 ml (3 fl oz) hot water in a cup.
2 Firmly tamp ground coffee to ensure that the water flow is restricted. Use a twin group head for an even extraction.
3 The pour/extraction should take about 30 seconds.
4 Serve in a standard ceramic or glass cup with a layer of golden caramel crema.

AMERICANO

A similar coffee is the Americano, which is made in reverse order to the long black – coffee first, water second.

This coffee originated during World War 2 when American girls would pour hot water into expresso to try and make it like the coffee they were used to back home.

Macchiato

90 ml (3 fl oz) cup
1 shot (30 ml/1 fl oz) espresso
1–2 teaspoons of hot or cold milk

"Macchiato" means marked or stained. Espresso macchiato is a single espresso "stained" with a small amount (1–2 teaspoons) of hot or cold milk, usually with a small amount of foamed milk on top. The foamed milk was traditionally added to show the beverage had a little milk in it, so it wasn't confused with an espresso on serving. This coffee can also be served as a long macchiato, that is, a double espresso stained with a small amount of hot or cold milk.

MACCHIATO

1 Firmly tamp ground coffee to ensure that the water flow is restricted.
2 The pour/extraction should take about 30 seconds.
3 Serve in a glass or ceramic cup with a layer of golden crema on top. Add a dash of hot or cold milk before serving.

NOTE To make long macchiato, prepare a double shot of coffee before staining it with milk.

LATTE MACCHIATO

Latte macchiato literally means "stained milk", where steamed white milk gets "stained" by the addition of espresso. Latte macchiato differs from a caffè latte in that the espresso is added to the milk, rather than the other way around; it features more foam, rather than just hot milk; only a half-shot or less of espresso is used; and the drink is usually layered, not mixed all together.

Piccolo Latte

90 ml (3 fl oz) cup
espresso (1 shot)
steamed milk, little foam

Piccolo latte is a variant of caffè latte. It is a single espresso
shot in a machiatto glass, which is then filled with steamed
milk in the same fashion as a caffè latte. This results in a
shorter, stronger latte with about 5 mm (⅕ in) of foam on
the top.

PICCOLO LATTE

1 Firmly tamp ground coffee.
2 The pour should be just under ½ of the glass.
3 Top with steamed milk that is hot enough to drink almost
   immediately rather than waiting for it to cool.
4 Scoop milk froth to the top of the glass.
5 Serve in a 90 ml (3 fl oz) cup or glass.

Caffè Latte

160 ml (5 ⅓ fl oz) cup
espresso (1 shot)
steamed milk

In Italy, the caffè latte is traditionally a breakfast
drink, prepared at home. Outside Italy it is a standard
(30 ml/1 fl oz) or double (60 ml/1 fl oz) shot espresso,
filled with steamed milk and a layer of foamed milk
(approx 12 mm/½ in) on top.

Caffè latte is an Italian term for a double serving of espresso
with steamed milk. Café au lait in French, café con leche in
Spanish and Kaffee mit Milch in German are the same thing.

The caffè latte serving is up to one-third espresso to
two-thirds steamed milk, served in a ceramic glass or a
wide-mouthed glass. Lattes are also served embellished
with different syrups (like vanilla or caramel) added before
espresso, or steamed with milk.

In Italy if you ordered a "latte" you would receive a glass
of milk.

CAFFÈ LATTE

1 Firmly tamp ground coffee.
2 The pour should be under ⅓ of the glass.
3 Add steamed milk that is hot enough to drink almost
   immediately rather than waiting for it to cool.
4 Scoop milk froth to the top of the glass.
5 Serve in a glass.

Flat White

160 ml (5⅓ fl oz) cup
espresso (1 shot)
steamed milk

The flat white originated in Australia and New Zealand during the early 1980s. It is prepared by pouring steamed milk from the bottom of a steaming jug over a single shot of espresso.

The drink is typically served in small ceramic cups. To achieve the flat, no-froth texture the steamed milk is poured from the bottom of the jug, holding back the lighter froth on top in order to access the milk with smaller bubbles, making the drink smooth and velvety in texture and keeping the crema intact.

FLAT WHITE

1 Firmly tamp ground coffee.
2 The pour/extraction should take about 30 seconds.
3 Add hot milk.
4 Serve in a ceramic cup.

Cappuccino

160 ml (5 ⅓ fl oz) cup
espresso (1 shot)
steamed milk
milk froth

The origin of the word "cappuccino" dates back over
500 years to the Capuchin order of friars. The order's
name derives from its long, pointed cowl or "cappuccino",
a derivative of "cappuccio" meaning "hood" in Italian. It has
long been debated as to the link between the Capuchin
monks and the cappuccino drink, but it is said that the coffee
was named after the friars because the coffee resembled
the paticular hue of their habit. The first use of the word
cappuccino in English was recorded in 1948.

CAPPUCCINO

1   Firmly tamp ground coffee.
2   The pour/extraction should take about 30 seconds.
3   Add hot milk to approximately 1.5 cm (⅗ in) below rim of
    cup.
4   Add milk froth, which can sit higher than the rim of
    the cup.
5   Garnish with a sprinkle of chocolate powder.
6   Serve in a cup or glass.

Mocha

160 ml (5 ⅓ fl oz) cup
espresso (1 shot)
steamed milk
1 teaspoon chocolate powder

Caffè mocha takes its name from the Red Sea coastal town of Mocha, Yemen, which as far back as the fifteenth century was a dominant exporter of coffee, especially to areas around the Arabian Peninsula.

A caffè mocha is a variant of a cappuccino. Like a cappuccino, it is typically is topped with approximately 2 cm (⅘ in) foam, but a portion of chocolate is added to the espresso shot, typically in the form of sweet cocoa powder, although many varieties use chocolate syrup. Mochas can contain dark or milk chocolate.

Like cappuccino, mochas contain the well-known milk froth on top, although they are sometimes served with whipped cream instead. They are usually topped with a dusting of either cinnamon or cocoa powder. Marshmallows may also be added on top for decoration.

A variant is white caffè mocha, made with white chocolate instead of milk or dark. There are also variants of the drink that mix the two syrups – this mixture is referred to by several names, including black and white mocha, tan mocha, tuxedo mocha and zebra.

MOCHA

1 Pour one teaspoon of drinking chocolate power in a coffee cup.
2 Firmly tamp ground coffee.
3 The pour/extraction should take about 30 seconds. Stir.
4 Top with steamed milk.
5 Sprinkle with chocolate powder.

Vienna Coffee

Legend has it that soldiers of the Polish-Habsburg army, while liberating Vienna from the second Turkish siege in 1683, came across a number of sacks of strange beans, which they first thought were camel feed and wanted to destroy. The Polish king granted the sacks to a Polish noble named Franz Georg Kolschitzky, who was instrumental in defeating the Turkish. He opened a coffee house called the Blue Bottle, and began serving coffee as it was prepared in Constantinople (a concoction of pulp and water). The Viennese did not take to this and, after experimentation, Kolschitzky decided to filter the coffee and add cream and honey. Success was immediate.

Vienna coffee is a popular cream-based coffee. It is made by preparing strong shots of espresso into a standard cup or glass and topping with cream (instead of milk or sugar). The coffee is consumed through the cream top.

VIENNA COFFEE
90 ml (3 fl oz) cup
2 shots espresso
whipped cream

---

1 Firmly tamp ground coffee.
2 The pour/extraction should take about 30 seconds.
3 Serve in a 90 ml (3 fl oz) glass with whipped cream on top and dusted with cocoa powder.

Iced Coffee

Iced coffee can be a refreshing afternoon treat. If it's really hot outside and you want to cool down but still need your caffeine hit, iced coffee is the way to go.

There are many variations of iced coffee, depending on which country you are in. Many Italian cafés serve caffè freddo, which is straight espresso kept in the freezer and served as a slushie.

In Australia, it is usually chilled coffee and milk with ice cream and/or whipped cream.

In Canada, it is known as an iced cappuccino or ice capp and it is a frozen coffee slushie mixed with cream.

In Greece, there is a variation called a frappé. It is whipped in an electric mixer to create the foam on top. Milk is optional.

Thai iced coffee is strong black coffee sweetened with sugar, heavy cream and cardamom, quickly cooled and served over ice.

Vietnamese iced coffee is drip coffee with condensed milk over ice.

Most countries also have commercial iced coffees available as well. These are usually sweetened milk drinks.

ICED COFFEE
400 ml (⅔ pint) glass
1 scoop ice cream
1-2 espresso shots
cold milk
whipped fresh cream

1   Prepare espresso shots.
2   Transfer the hot coffee to a carafe or pitcher.
3   Refrigerate until cold, about 2–3 hours.
4   Add 1 scoop of ice cream in a tall or milkshake glass.
5   Add cold coffee to glass until half-full – for a weaker serve add less coffee.
6   Pour cold milk to 1 cm (²/₅ in) under the brim of the glass and stir a couple of times.
7   Finish with whipped cream and garnish with chocolate powder and coffee beans.

Iced Chocolate

Iced chocolate is a wonderful way to get your chocolate fix in hot weather – when a hot chocolate just won't do!

ICED CHOCOLATE
400 ml (⅔ pint) glass
2 tablespoons drinking chocolate
cold milk
whipped cream and ice cream

---

1 Mix the desired amount of drinking chocolate with a little hot water or milk to make a smooth, thick liquid.
2 Drizzle the liquid decoratively around the inside of a tall glass.
3 Add some ice.
4 Pour cold milk to 1 cm (⅖ in) under the brim of the glass.
5 Top with whipped cream and ice cream and dust with chocolate powder.

A variation of this drink is the iced mocha, where chilled coffee is added.

ICED MOCHA

---

1 Prepare 1-2 espresso shots.
2 The pour/extraction should take about 30 seconds.
3 Combine the hot coffee and 1½ tablespoons brown sugar in a large measuring cup and stir until the brown sugar dissolves. Stir in chocolate syrup. Transfer to a a carafe or pitcher.
4 Refrigerate until cold, about 2–3 hours.
5 Combine the chilled coffee, ice-cold milk, and ¼ teaspoon vanilla extract. Stir to blend. Pour into glass, adding a small handful of crushed ice.
6 Finish with whipped cream and ice cream and garnish with grated chocolate.

Hot Chocolate

Hot chocolate is a heated beverage typically consisting of shaved chocolate, melted chocolate buds or cocoa powder, heated milk or water, and sugar.

Drinking chocolate is similar to hot chocolate (or cocoa), but is made from melted chocolate shavings or paste rather than a powdered mix that's soluble in water.

The first chocolate beverage is believed to have been created by the Mayan peoples around 2000 years ago, and a cocoa beverage was an essential part of Aztec culture by 1400 AD. The beverage became popular in Europe after being introduced from Mexico, and has undergone multiple changes since then. Until the 19th century, hot chocolate was even used medicinally to treat ailments such as stomach diseases. Today, hot chocolate is consumed throughout the world and comes in multiple variations including the very thick, dense chocolate served in Italy.

Ceramic or glass cup
1 tablespoon drinking chocolate
hot milk to fill the cup

HOT CHOCOLATE

1   Mix 1 tablespoon drinking chocolate in a mug with a little hot water or milk to make a smooth, thick liquid.
2   Fill mug with hot frothed milk and sprinkle with chocolate. Serve with marshmallow if desired.

ITALIAN HOT CHOCOLATE

1   Mix 4 tbsp unsweetened cocoa, 3 tbsp sugar and ½ teaspoon arrowroot together until thoroughly blended.

2   Add 60 ml (2 fl oz) milk to a medium saucepan and set over low heat. Whisk in the cocoa mixture until thoroughly incorporated and no lumps remain. Add 180 ml (6 fl oz) of milk.

3   Cook, stirring constantly, over medium-low heat, until the mixture is thickened, about 10 minutes.

4   Once the cocoa has thickened, stir in and further additions you would like before serving – ⅛ teaspoon vanilla or almond extract or a teaspoon of Grand Marnier would be nice. Dust with cinnamon or nutmeg.

Note Alternatively, you can substitute half the liquid with coffee to make a nice mocha.

Babycino

A babycino (also known as a steamer) is a drink of frothed milk but no coffee. It is primarily marketed towards children. It can have syrups added, or be topped with chocolate sprinkle or marshmallows. It is usually served to small children in a short black cup.

BABYCINO

1   Drizzle syrup decoratively around the inside of a glass.
2   Fill glass with hot or warm frothed milk.
3   Add marshmallow if desired.
4   Sprinkle with chocolate powder.

• Coffee syrups

The early 1990s saw the growth of boutique coffee and with this came the increased usage of specialty syrups, such as vanilla and caramel, to add taste to lattes and other hot drinks. It was around this time that companies began to develop syrup that retain taste and consistency in hot drinks such as lattes and mochas, while also being just as tasty in cold drinks such as cocktails and Italian sodas. Now syrups are an essential part of any drink menu, and offer a powerful tool for reaching customers. The category continues to grow and invites non-coffee drinkers or new entrants into the market. Syrups are fun, easy to use and offer endless ways to enhance menus and drinks. When using syrup in a hot drink, make sure you add the syrup first, and extract your coffee into the syrup – this will both activate the taste of the syrup and make sure it is evenly dispersed throughout the cup.

Chai Latte

WHAT IS CHAI TEA?

Chai, pronounced with a long "i" as in the word tie, is the actual word for tea in many countries. Chai tea is quickly becoming extremely popular in the West as people are becoming exposed to it in coffee and tea houses.

Chai tea is a rich and complex beverage that has been enjoyed for centuries in many parts of the world, especially India. In its most basic form, chai is black tea that is brewed strong with a combination of spices, then diluted with milk and sugar.

The spices vary from recipe to recipe, but usually consist of cinnamon, cardamom, cloves, pepper and ginger. Chai tea is traditionally consumed hot and sweet. The sweetness is needed to bring out the full depth of the spices.

A chai latte is just the spiced tea mixed with milk steamed from an espresso machine.

CHAI LATTE

1   Place 180 ml (6 fl oz) water, 1 stick of cinnamon, 4 cardamom pods, 4 whole cloves, and 5 mm (⅕ in) fresh ginger root (thinly sliced) in a pot and bring to the boil.
2   Cover, lower heat and simmer for 10 minutes.
3   Add 3 teaspoons sugar and again bring to simmer.
4   Add 1½ teaspoons of tea leaves, remove from heat and cover.
5   Let steep for 3 minutes, then strain.
6   Top with steamed milk that is hot enough to drink almost immediately rather than waiting for it to cool.
7   Scoop milk froth to the top of the glass.

Coffee Drinks

In this chapter we have developed a very
tasty series of coffee drinks, most of them
including a selected liqueur, designed for
that "after a great meal" mellow feeling.

Affogato Agave

Makes 1

PREPARATION 5 minutes

---

2 scoops vanilla bean ice cream
45 ml (1½ fl oz) espresso coffee
45 ml (1½ fl oz) Patron XO Café Tequila, Frangelico
   or Kahlúa
1 teaspoon hazelnuts, chopped

---

1   Put the ice cream in the glass and drown it with the
    espresso coffee.
2   Pour over your choice of liqueur.
3   Garnish with chopped hazelnuts.

Café Agave

Makes 1

PREPARATION 5 minutes

---

45 ml (1½ fl oz) Patron XO Café Tequila
45 ml (1½ fl oz) cocoa liqueur
60 ml (2 fl oz) espresso coffee
60 ml (2 fl oz) cream
1 chocolate flake

---

1   Shake all ingredients, except chocolate flakes, with ice
    and strain into the glass.
2   Serve in martini glass, garnished with chocolate flakes.

Caribbean Coffee

Makes 1

PREPARATION 5 minutes

---

45 ml (1½ fl oz) dark rum
150 ml (5 fl oz) hot black coffee/one long black coffee
3 tablespoons whipped cream

---

1 Pour rum and coffee into an Irish coffee cup and sweeten
   to taste.
2 Float the cream on top, sprinkle with grated chocolate,
   and serve.
2 Garnish with chocolate-coated coffee beans.

VARIATIONS

Alternatively, you can make this by substituting Kahlúa for
the dark rum.

Blackjack

Makes 1

PREPARATION 5 minutes

45 ml (1½ fl oz) Kirsch
60 ml (2 fl oz) fresh coffee
2 teaspoons brandy

1 Stir all ingredients with crushed ice in a mixing glass, strain, then pour into cocktail glass.
2 Serve garnished with coffee granules.

VARIATIONS

Alternatively, you can make *Roulette* by substituting vodka for Kirsch.

Café Oscar

Makes 1

PREPARATION 5 minutes

---

20 ml (⅔ fl oz) Kahlúa
20 ml (⅔ fl oz) Amaretto
hot coffee
double cream
1 scoop vanilla ice cream

---

1 Pour spirits into glass, then top up with coffee.
2 Float cream on top. Garnish with ice cream.

VARIATIONS

Alternatively, you can make *Café Maria* by substituting
Tia Maria and Galliano for Kahlúa and Amaretto.

Irish Coffee

Makes 1

PREPARATION 5 minutes

---

1 teaspoon brown sugar
45 ml (1½ fl oz) Baileys
hot black coffee
45 ml (1½ fl oz) fresh whipped cream
chocolate flakes or chocolate powder

---

1   Stir sugar into Baileys. Top up with coffee. Float fresh
     cream on top, then garnish with chocolate.

VARIATIONS

Alternatively, you can make Irish coffee with whiskey by
substituting a good Irish whiskey such as Tullamore Dew
or Jameson's for the Baileys. Other liqueur coffees are:
French – brandy, English – gin, Russian – vodka, American
– Bourbon, Calypso – dark rum, Jamaican – Tia Maria,
Parisienne – Grand Marnier, Mexican – Kahlúa, Monks –
Benedictine, Scottish – Scotch, Canadian – rye.

Coffee Break

Makes 1

PREPARATION 5 minutes

---

125 ml (4 fl oz) hot black coffee
20 ml (⅔ fl oz) brandy
20 ml (⅔ fl oz) Kahlúa
60 ml (3 fl oz) whipped cream
1 maraschino cherry

---

1 Pour coffee and liquors into an Irish coffee cup and
   sweeten to taste.
2 Float the cream on top, add a maraschino cherry,
   and serve.

VARIATIONS

Alternatively, you can make *Peppermint Break* by
substituting crème de menthe for brandy.

Coffee Nudge

Makes 1

PREPARATION 5 minutes

2 teaspoons dark crème de cacao
2 teaspoons Kahlúa
20 ml (⅔ fl oz) brandy
1 cup hot coffee
60 ml (2 fl oz) whipped cream

1   Combine liquors with coffee and top with whipped cream.

VARIATIONS

Alternatively, you can make *Liquorice Coffee* by substituting black sambuca for the brandy and coffee liqueur.

Iced Cappuccino

Makes 1

PREPARATION 5 minutes

---

90 ml (3 fl oz) strong espresso
60 ml (2 fl oz) milk
45 ml (1½ fl oz) vanilla syrup
20 ml (⅔ fl oz) Kahlúa
20 ml (⅔ fl oz) caramel syrup
60 ml (2 fl oz) cream

---

1   Blend all ingredients with 2 scoops of ice. Pour into a
    poco grande glass.

Mocha Mudslide Milkshake

Makes 1

PREPARATION 5 minutes

---

250 ml (8 fl oz) milk
1 small sliced ripe banana
45 ml (1½ fl oz) sugar
30 ml (1 fl oz) espresso
120 ml (4 fl oz) vanilla yoghurt

---

1   Place the milk, banana, sugar and espresso in a blender and blend until smooth. Freeze in a blender container for 1 hour or until slightly frozen. Loosen frozen mixture from the sides of blender container, add yoghurt and blend until smooth. Garnish with extra banana slices. Serve immediately.

Galliano Hotshot

Makes 1

PREPARATION 5 minutes

---

20 ml (⅔ fl oz) Galliano
20 ml (⅔ fl oz) hot coffee
20 ml (⅔ fl oz) double cream

---

1   Pour the Galliano into a shot glass, then carefully pour the coffee on top. Finally, gently spoon the cream on top of the coffee layer.

Royale Coffee

Makes 1

PREPARATION 5 minutes

45 ml (1½ fl oz) Cognac
150 ml (5 fl oz) hot black coffee
60 ml (2 fl oz) whipped cream
1 teaspoon grated chocolate

1   Add coffee and Cognac to an Irish coffee cup and
    sweeten to taste. Gently float whipped cream on top,
    sprinkle with grated chocolate, and serve.

Coffee Biscuits

Nothing better than a little finisher with coffee, a biscuit or "petits fours". We have developed some very tasty biscuits in this chapter, from heavier chocolate-based biscuits to very light "Coffee Kisses". Try these easy to make and much easier to eat recipes, we know you will enjoy the sensation.

Coffee Choc Bit Biscuits

Makes 18

PREPARATION 15 minutes COOKING 15 minutes

---

120 g (4 oz) butter
110 g (3⅔ oz) caster sugar
100 g (3⅓ oz) brown sugar, firmly packed
4 teaspoons instant coffee
1 egg
270 g (9 oz) self-raising flour
1 cup choc bits

---

1 Preheat oven to 180°C (360°F).
2 Cream butter and sugars. Beat in coffee, then egg.
3 Stir in flour and choc chip bits until mixed.
4 Drop spoonfuls of mixture onto a greased baking tray and bake for 10–15 minutes. Allow to cool on tray.

Mocha Meringues

Makes 12

PREPARATION 1 hour 15 minutes COOKING 40 minutes

1 egg white
⅛ teaspoon cream of tartar
65 g (2⅓ oz) white sugar
¼ teaspoon vanilla extract
10 g (⅓ oz) cocoa powder
½ teaspoon instant coffee powder

1   Preheat oven to 120°C (250°F).
2   Beat egg white and cream of tartar at high speed until
    soft peaks form. Gradually add sugar, vanilla, cocoa,
    and coffee.
3   Drop mixture onto a foil-lined baking sheet in 12 mounds.
    They should be about 5 cm (2 in) apart.
4   Bake for 40 minutes or until firm. Turn off oven and let
    meringues cool in oven for 1 hour. Do not open oven door
    while the meringues are cooling.

Coffee Kisses

Makes 25

PREPARATION 12 minutes   COOKING 12 minutes

---

250 g (8⅓ oz) butter, at room temperature
80 g (2⅔ oz) icing (confectioner's) sugar, sifted
2 teaspoons instant coffee powder,
    dissolved in 4 teaspoons hot water, then cooled
300 g (10 oz) plain flour, sifted
bittersweet chocolate, melted

---

1 Preheat oven to 180°C (360°F).
2 Place the butter and icing sugar in a bowl and beat until light and fluffy. Stir in the coffee mixture and flour.
3 Spoon the mixture into a piping bag fitted with a medium star nozzle and pipe 2.5 cm (1 in) rounds of mixture 2.5 cm (1 in) apart on greased baking trays. Bake for 10–12 minutes or until lightly browned. Stand on trays for 5 minutes before removing to wire racks to cool completely.
4 Join the biscuits with a little melted chocolate, then dust with icing sugar.

Note These coffee biscuits have a similar texture to shortbread, making the dough perfect for piping. For something different, pipe 5 cm (2 in) lengths instead of rounds. Rather than sandwiching the biscuits together with chocolate, you may prefer to leave them plain and simply dust with icing sugar.

Chocolate Melting Moments

Makes 13 pairs

PREPARATION 10 minutes   COOKING 20 minutes

250 g (8⅓ oz) butter, at room temperature
80 g (2⅔ oz) icing (confectioner's) sugar, sifted
2 teaspoons vanilla extract
225 g (7½ oz) plain flour
3 tablespoons cocoa powder
30 g (1 oz) cornflour

CHOCOLATE CREAM
50 g (1½ oz) butter, at room temperature
4 teaspoons cocoa powder
½ teaspoon vanilla extract
1 teaspoon instant coffee powder
120 g (4 oz) icing sugar

1   Preheat oven to 180°C (360°F).
2   Beat butter and icing sugar together until fluffy.
3   Add vanilla. Sift in flour, cocoa and cornflour. Beat with a wooden spoon to combine.
4   Measure spoonfuls of mixture onto a greased oven tray. Flatten with a fork.
5   Bake for 15–20 minutes.
6   Cool on a wire rack. Sandwich together with chocolate cream.

CHOCOLATE CREAM

1   Place butter in a bowl. Beat in cocoa, vanilla, coffee and icing sugar until smooth.

Coffee Pecan Biscuits

Makes 30

PREPARATION 40 minutes   COOKING 18 minutes

125 g (4 oz) butter, at room temperature
120 g (4 oz) caster sugar
½ teaspoon vanilla extract
1 egg, at room temperature
2 teaspoons instant coffee powder
300 g (10 oz) plain flour
1 teaspoon baking powder
4 teaspoons milk
250 g (8 oz) pecans, finely chopped

COFFEE ICING
120 g (4 oz) icing (confectioner's) sugar
4 teaspoons boiling water
4 teaspoons butter, at room temperature
2 teaspoons instant coffee powder

1   Using an electric mixer, beat butter, sugar and vanilla in
    a small bowl until pale and creamy. Add egg and coffee
    and mix until well combined. Sift flour and baking powder
    over butter mixture. Add milk and stir until just combined.
    Divide dough in half.
2   Roll each piece of dough into a 5 cm (2 in) diameter log.
    Roll the logs in the chopped pecans until well coated.
    Wrap each log in cling wrap. Refrigerate for at least
    30 minutes or until firm.
3   Preheat oven to 180°C (360°F). Line 2 baking trays with
    baking paper.
4   Using a sharp knife, carefully cut logs into 15 mm (½ in)
    slices.

5   Place on the lined baking trays. Bake for 15–18 minutes or until light golden brown. Allow to cool for about 5 minutes, then transfer to wire racks to cool completely.
6   Make coffee icing. Sift icing sugar into a bowl. Combine the boiling water, butter and coffee in a separate bowl and stir until coffee is dissolved. Add to icing sugar and stir until mixture is smooth.
7   Drop 1 teaspoon of icing onto the centre of each biscuit. Top with a pecan. Allow icing to set before serving.

Bourbon Biscuits

Makes 14–16

PREPARATION 30 minutes   COOKING 20 minutes

---

60 g (2 oz) butter
60 g (2 oz) caster sugar
4 teaspoons golden syrup
150 g (5 oz) plain flour
15 g (½ oz) cocoa powder
½ teaspoon baking soda

FILLING
50 g (1½ oz) butter
105 g (3½ oz) icing (confectioner's) sugar, sifted
4 teaspoons cocoa powder
1 teaspoon instant coffee powder

---

1   Preheat the oven to 160°C (320°F). Cream the butter and
    sugar together very thoroughly, then beat in the syrup.
2   Sift the flour, cocoa and baking soda together, then work
    into the creamed mixture to make a stiff paste.
3   Knead well, and roll out on a lightly floured surface into
    an oblong strip about 5 mm (⅕ in) thick. If the rolled
    dough is too long for your baking tray, cut it in half.
    Place on a lightly buttered baking tray covered with
    baking paper. Bake for 15–20 minutes.
4   Cut into fingers of equal width while still warm. Cool on a
    wire rack while you prepare the filling.

FILLING

---

1   Beat the butter until soft, then add the sugar, cocoa and
    coffee. Beat until smooth. Sandwich the cooled fingers
    with a layer of filling.

Brazilian Coffee Biscuits

Makes 24

PREPARATION 20 minutes COOKING 10 minutes

---

100 g (3½ oz) butter
100 g (3½ oz) soft dark brown sugar
100 g (3½ oz) caster sugar
1 egg
1 ½ teaspoons vanilla extract
4 teaspoons milk
330 g (11 oz) plain flour
½ teaspoon salt
¼ teaspoon baking soda
¼ teaspoon baking powder
8 teaspoons instant coffee powder

---

1 Preheat oven to 200°C (390°F). Line baking trays with baking paper.
2 Beat the butter, brown sugar, caster sugar, egg, vanilla and milk until fluffy.
3 In a separate bowl, mix the flour, salt, baking soda, baking powder and instant coffee. Add to sugar mixture and mix thoroughly.
4 Shape dough in 2.5 cm (1 in) balls. If too soft to shape, chill for a while. Place balls 5 cm (2 in) apart on baking trays.
5 Flatten to 1 cm (½ in) thickness with fork or glass dipped in sugar. Bake for 8–10 minutes until lightly browned.

Macadamia Coconut Squares

Makes 48

PREPARATION 30 minutes COOKING 1 hour 10 minutes

---

250 g (8 oz) butter
440 g (1 lb) brown sugar, firmly packed
4 teaspoons instant coffee powder
½ teaspoon ground cinnamon
½ teaspoon salt
300 g (10 oz) plain flour
3 eggs
2 teaspoons vanilla extract
150 g (5 oz) desiccated coconut
300 g (10 oz) chopped toasted macadamias

---

1 Preheat oven to 170°C (340°F).
2 Lightly butter a 22 x 33 cm (8½ x 13 in) baking pan and set aside.
3 In a large mixing bowl, beat butter, half the brown sugar, instant coffee powder, half of the cinnamon and half of the salt until light and fluffy. Stir in flour a little at a time, blending well after each addition.
4 Spread evenly in prepared pan. Bake for 20 minutes. Cool in pan on rack for 15 minutes.
5 In a large bowl, beat eggs and vanilla with remaining brown sugar, cinnamon and salt. Stir in coconut and macadamias. Spread evenly over cooled baked layer.
6 Bake for 40–50 minutes, or until golden brown and firm to the touch. Use a knife to loosen around edges while warm.
7 Cool completely in pan on a rack. Cut into 48 squares, cutting 6 strips one way and 8 strips the other way.
8 Store in an airtight container at room temperature.

Cappuccino Crisps

Makes about 75

PREPARATION 1 hour   COOKING 10 minutes

250 g (8 oz) unsalted butter
220 g (7½ oz) white sugar
60 g (2 oz) cocoa powder
¼ teaspoon ground cinnamon
1 egg
2 teaspoons instant coffee powder
1 teaspoon vanilla extract
300 g (10 oz) plain flour

ICING
320 g (11 oz) icing (confectioner's) sugar
60 ml (2 fl oz) hot milk
60 g (2 oz) butter
4 teaspoons golden syrup
2 teaspoons instant coffee powder
1 teaspoon vanilla extract
1 teaspoon olive oil
¼ teaspoon salt

1   Beat butter, sugar, cocoa and cinnamon in a large bowl,
    then beat in the egg.
2   Stir coffee powder, vanilla and 1 teaspoon water in a cup
    to dissolve coffee. Beat into butter mixture.
3   On low speed, beat in flour just until blended.
    Divide dough in half and shape into disks. Wrap and chill
    until firm.
4   Preheat oven to 190°C (375°F). Have ready a 75 mm
    (3 in) star cookie cutter.
5   Roll dough on a well-floured surface to about 5 mm

(¼ in) thickness. Cut out stars and place 25 mm (1 in) apart on an ungreased cookie sheet.

6   Bake for 8 minutes or until crisp.

7   To make the icing, put icing sugar in a medium bowl, gradually stir in hot milk until smooth, stir in butter until blended, then add remaining ingredients and 1 tablespoon hot water. Spoon icing into a corner of a plastic bag, snip off the tip of the corner and drizzle zigzag design on cookies.

Chocolate Coffee Tuiles

Makes 25

PREPARATION 20 minutes COOKING 5 minutes

---

2 egg whites
110 g (3½ oz) caster sugar
½ teaspoon instant coffee powder,
    dissolved in ½ teaspoon water
1 teaspoon vanilla extract
4 teaspoons cocoa powder, sifted
5 teaspoons milk
60 g butter (2 oz), melted and cooled

---

1 Preheat oven to 170°C (340°F).
2 Place egg whites in a bowl and beat until soft peaks form.
   Gradually add sugar, beating well after each addition,
   until mixture is glossy and sugar dissolved. Fold coffee
   mixture, vanilla, cocoa powder, milk and butter into egg
   white mixture.
3 Drop spoonfuls of mixture 10 cm (4 in) apart onto
   greased baking tray and bake for 5 minutes or until
   edges are set. Remove from tray and wrap each biscuit
   around the handle of a wooden spoon. Allow to cool for
   2 minutes or until set. Repeat with remaining mixture.

Coffee Biscuits

Makes 12

PREPARATION 15 minutes   COOKING 30 minutes

---

110 g (3½ oz) butter
85 g (3 oz) sugar
1 egg
1 teaspoon coffee essence
225 g (7½ oz) self-raising flour

COFFEE ICING
45 g (1½ oz) butter, softened
105 g (3½ oz) icing (confectioner's) sugar
2 teaspoons instant coffee powder

---

1   Preheat oven to 180°C (360°F).
2   Cream butter and sugar. Add egg and beat well.
    Add coffee essence and flour and combine well.
3   Roll into balls and flatten with a fork.
4   Bake for 30 minutes. When cold, join with coffee icing.

COFFEE ICING

---

1   Beat butter, icing sugar and coffee together until smooth.

Coffee Cakes

"Coffee and cake", now that sounds inviting. In this chapter we have developed some terrific recipes, designed to be served with great coffee. All of the recipes are easy to make, yet will give you the results you wish to achieve.

Cappuccino Cheesecake

Makes 12 slices

PREPARATION 30 minutes   COOKING 1 hour 20 minutes

BASE
225 g (7½ oz) finely chopped nuts (almonds, walnuts)
30 g (1 oz) sugar
60 g (2 oz) butter, melted

FILLING
1 kg (2¼ pounds) cream cheese, at room temperature
225 g (7½ oz) sugar
12 teaspoons plain flour
4 large eggs
250 ml (8 fl oz) sour cream
4 teaspoons instant coffee powder
¼ teaspoon ground cinnamon

---

1   Preheat oven to 160°C (320°F).

BASE
2   Combine nuts, sugar and butter, press onto bottom of
    23 cm (9 in) springform tin. Bake for 10 minutes, remove
    from oven and allow to cool. Increase oven temperature
    to 230°C (445°F).

FILLING
3   Combine cream cheese, sugar and flour in an electric
    mixer, mix on medium speed until well blended.
    Add eggs, one at a time, mixing well after each addition.
    Blend in sour cream.

4   Dissolve coffee and cinnamon in 60 ml (2 fl oz) boiling water. Cool, then gradually add to cream cheese mixture, mixing until well blended. Pour over base.
5   Bake for 10 minutes. Reduce oven temperature to 120°C (250°F) and continue baking for 1 hour.
6   Loosen cake from rim, allow to cool before removing. Chill. Serve topped with whipped cream and coffee beans.

Cocomo Cheesecake

Makes 12 slices

PREPARATION 30 minutes   COOKING 1 hour 15 minutes

BASE
120 g (4 oz) digestive biscuits, finely crushed
45 g (1½ oz) sugar
60 g (1 oz) butter, melted

FILLING
60 g (2 oz) cooking chocolate
45 g (1½ oz) butter
500 g (1 lb) cream cheese, at room temperature
270 g (9 oz) sugar
5 large eggs
60 g (2 oz) flaked coconut

TOPPING
250 ml (8 fl oz) sour cream
30 g (1 oz) sugar
30 ml (1 fl oz) passionfruit liqueur
1 teaspoon instant coffee powder

---

1   Preheat oven to 175°C (345°F).

BASE
2   Combine crumbs, sugar and butter, press onto bottom of
    23 cm (9 in) springform tin. Bake for 10 minutes.

FILLING
3   Melt chocolate and butter over low heat, stirring
    until smooth.
4   Combine cream cheese and sugar in an electric mixer,

mix on medium speed until well blended. Add eggs one at a time, mixing well after each addition. Blend in chocolate mixture and coconut, pour over base.

5   Bake for 60 minutes or until set.

TOPPING

6   Combine sour cream, sugar, liqueur and coffee, spread over cheesecake.

7   Reduce heat to 150°C (300°F) and bake for 5 minutes.

8   Loosen cake from rim of tin, cool before removing. Chill and serve dusted with cocoa powder.

Coffee and Walnut Surprises

Makes 12

PREPARATION 20 minutes   COOKING 20 minutes

---

250 g (8 oz) butter, at room temperature
105 g (3½ oz) sugar
2 eggs
45 ml (1½ fl oz) Baileys Irish Cream
105 g (3½ oz) chopped walnuts
8 teaspoons instant coffee powder
225 g (7½ oz) self-raising flour
icing (confectioner's) sugar

SAUCE
105 g (3½ oz) caster sugar
240 ml (8 fl oz) thickened cream
4 teaspoons instant coffee powder

---

1 Preheat oven to 180°C (360°F).
2 Beat butter and sugar until light and fluffy, stir in eggs, Baileys and walnuts. Sift in coffee and flour and mix to combine.
3 Divide mixture evenly into a lightly buttered 12-hole muffin or friand tin.
4 Bake for 15–20 minutes or until risen and firm.
5 Leave to cool for 10 minutes, then remove from tin. Pour over sauce. Serve with tea or coffee and Irish cream liqueur.

SAUCE

1 Heat sugar and 60 ml (2 fl oz) water in saucepan until mixture is boiling and sugar dissolves. Reduce heat, simmer until golden. Add cream and coffee. Bring to the boil and simmer until toffee dissolves and sauce thickens.

Espresso Cake

Serves 8–10

PREPARATION 30 minutes   COOKING 1 hour

½ cup finely ground espresso coffee beans
200 g (6½ oz) butter
270 g (9 oz) sugar
3 eggs
4 teaspoons vanilla extract
300 g (10 oz) plain flour
3 teaspoons baking powder

COFFEE CREAM
300 ml (10 fl oz) thickened cream
4 teaspoons icing (confectioner's) sugar
45 ml (1½ fl oz) very strong espresso coffee

---

1   Preheat oven to 180°C (360°F).
2   Pour 250 ml (8 fl oz) boiling water over half the
    ground coffee beans and leave to steep for 5 minutes.
    Strain liquid from beans and pour over butter in a
    large bowl, stirring until butter melts. Discard the
    strained beans.
3   Mix in sugar, eggs and vanilla and beat with a wooden
    spoon until combined. Sift flour and baking powder into
    mixture and mix in with remaining ground coffee beans.
4   Pour the mixture into a baking-paper-lined 20 cm (8 in)
    square cake tin. Bake for 50–55 minutes or until cake
    springs back when lightly touched.
5   Cool in tin for 10 minutes before turning onto a cooling
    rack. Dust with cinnamon and serve with coffee cream.
6   To make the coffee cream, whip cream until soft, then
    beat in icing sugar and coffee.

Modern Anzac Cake

Serves 12–16

PREPARATION 30 minutes   COOKING 1 hour 20 minutes

125 g (4 oz) butter, at room temperature
200 g (6½ oz) sugar
2 eggs
1 teaspoon vanilla extract
90 g (3 oz) ground almonds
12 teaspoons cocoa powder
30 g (1 oz) shredded coconut
200 g (6½ oz) self-raising flour
315 g (10½ oz) sour cream
125 ml (4 fl oz) espresso coffee

TOPPING
210 g (7 oz) sugar
75 ml (2½ fl oz) golden syrup
75 g (2½ oz) butter
150 g (5 oz) flaked almonds
30 g (1 oz) shredded coconut
30 g (1 oz) rolled oats

1   Preheat the oven to 160°C (320°F) and butter and line a
    24 cm (10 in) cake tin.
2   Cream the butter and sugar together until thick and pale,
    then add the eggs one at a time, beating well after each
    addition. Add the vanilla and mix well to combine.
3   In a separate bowl, mix together the almonds, cocoa,
    coconut and flour.
4   Fold half the flour mixture into the batter with the sour
    cream and combine gently. Add the remaining flour
    mixture with the coffee and mix well.

5 Bake in the preheated oven for 1 hour until puffed and cooked through.

6 Meanwhile, prepare the topping. Place 150 ml (5 fl oz) water and the sugar in a small saucepan and heat gently while stirring to dissolve the sugar granules. When the mixture begins to boil, stop stirring and simmer for about 5 minutes, brushing down the sides of the pan with a pastry brush. When the mixture is pale gold, remove from the heat and stir in the golden syrup, butter, almonds, coconut and rolled oats and stir thoroughly, returning to the heat if necessary to help you mix the ingredients well. After the cake has cooked for 1 hour, remove from the oven and pour this mixture over the cake, then return to the oven for 10 minutes or until the topping has set.

7 Remove the cake from the oven and allow to cool in the tin for 10 minutes. Use a knife to loosen any toffee from the sides of the tin, then remove the cake and cool completely on a wire rack. Serve as a superb winter dessert.

Sticky Date Cupcakes

Makes 12

PREPARATION 12 minutes   COOKING 20 minutes

---

2 eggs
135 g (4½ oz) butter, at room temperature
(5½ oz) caster sugar
150 g (5 oz) self-raising flour, sifted
400 g (14 oz) dates, chopped
2 teaspoons instant coffee powder
1 teaspoon baking soda
1 teaspoon vanilla extract
105 g (3½ oz) ground almond flour
60 g (2 oz) walnuts, finely chopped

TOPPING
210 g (7 oz) light-brown sugar, firmly packed
60 g (2 oz) unsalted butter
1 teaspoon vanilla extract
250 ml (8 fl oz) whipped cream
12 dates

---

1   Preheat the oven to 160°C (320°F). Line a 12-cupcake
    pan with cupcake papers. In a bowl, lightly beat the eggs,
    add the butter and sugar, then mix until light and fluffy.
2   Add 180 ml (6 fl oz) water and the flour, and stir to
    combine. Add remaining ingredients. Mix with a wooden
    spoon for 2 minutes, until light and creamy.
3   Divide the mixture evenly between the cake papers.
    Bake for 18–20 minutes until risen and firm to touch.
    Allow to cool for a few minutes and then transfer to a
    wire rack. Allow to cool fully before icing.

TOPPING

1 Meanwhile, combine sugar, butter, vanilla and
   1 tablespoon water in a saucepan. Bring to a simmer over
   medium-low heat, stirring constantly. Without stirring
   again, simmer for 1 minute. Remove from heat and
   allow to cool. Fold through whipped cream. Spoon onto
   cupcakes and top with dates.

Torta Tiramisu

Serves 8–10

PREPARATION 1 hour   COOKING 45 minutes

---

6 egg whites
pinch of salt
230 g (7½ oz) caster sugar
100 g (3½ oz) roasted almonds, ground
1 tablespoon icing (confectioner's) sugar
45 g (1½ oz) cornflour

FILLING
7 level teaspoons gelatine
125 mL (4 fl oz) coffee liqueur
125 g (4 oz) caster sugar
45 g (1½ oz) instant coffee powder
500 g (1 lb) mascarpone cheese
4 egg yolks
250 ml (8 fl oz) thickened cream, whipped
80 (2½ oz) dark chocolate, finely grated
cocoa powder, for dusting

---

1 Preheat the oven to 180°C (360°F). Lightly butter and line
   two 24 cm (10 in) springform tins.
2 Firstly, make the meringue bases. Beat the egg whites
   and salt until stiff peaks form and then gradually add
   the caster sugar, a little at a time. Beat at top speed for
   10 minutes until the sugar is completely dissolved and the
   mixture is thick and glossy.
3 In a separate bowl, mix the almonds, icing sugar and
   cornflour, then gently fold into the egg white mixture.
   Divide the mixture evenly between the cake tins and bake
   at 180°C (360°F) for 45 minutes, then cool completely.

(If you do not have two 24 cm cake tins, bake half the mixture and, when cool, remove from the tin. Re-butter and line the cake tin to bake the remaining mixture.)

4   Place the gelatine and 60 ml (2 fl oz) water in a small bowl and stand in a pan of boiling water to dissolve, or heat in a microwave oven on high for 10 seconds. Place the coffee liqueur, sugar and instant coffee in a saucepan and bring to the boil. Stir in the dissolved gelatine and mix well. Set aside. Place the mascarpone in a mixing bowl and beat in the egg yolks and coffee mixture. Gently fold in the whipped cream and mix gently.

5   To assemble the cake, place one of the meringue bases in the bottom of a 23 cm (9 in) springform pan and pour over half the filling. Smooth, then sprinkle with half the grated chocolate. Top with the second base and press down lightly. Cover with remaining filling and remaining chocolate. Chill for at least 2 hours. Carefully remove from the sides of the cake tin, then slide the cake off the base. Dust the top of the cake with cocoa powder.

Mocha Mousse Roll

Serves 8

PREPARATION 40 minutes   COOKING 30 minutes

180 g (6 oz) dark chocolate, grated
60 g (2 oz) butter
5 eggs, separated
45 ml (1½ fl oz) Tia Maria liqueur
75 g (2½ oz) caster sugar
8 teaspoons cocoa powder, sifted
4 teaspoons instant coffee powder
250 ml (8 fl oz) thickened cream

1   Preheat oven to 180°C (360°F). Lightly butter and line
    with baking paper a Swiss roll tin.
2   Melt chocolate and butter in a bowl over a bowl of
    simmering water and stir until smooth.
3   Beat in egg yolks one at a time, beating well after each
    addition. Stir in Tia Maria.
4   Beat egg whites in a small bowl until soft peaks form.
    Gradually add sugar, beating until mixture becomes
    thick and glossy. Fold in chocolate mixture, stir until
    well combined.
5   Spread mixture evenly into the Swiss roll tin. Bake for
    30 minutes until firm. Turn out onto a sheet of grease
    proof paper, sprinkle with sifted cocoa. Remove paper
    lining and allow to cool.
6   Combine coffee and 1 tablespoon boiling water, then
    cool. Beat cream until soft peaks form, stir in coffee
    mixture and 1 tablespoon extra Tia Maria. Spread evenly
    over cake and roll up lengthwise, using paper to help.
    Refrigerate until firm, then serve sliced.

Coffee Sandwich Cake

Serves 6–8

PREPARATION 1 hour   COOKING 35 minutes

250 g (8 oz) butter, at room temperature
220 g (7½ oz) caster sugar
6 eggs, lightly beaten
300 g (10 oz) self-raising flour, sifted

ICING
60 g (oz) butter, softened
120 g (4 oz) icing (confectioner's) sugar, sifted
½ teaspoon ground cinnamon
2 teaspoons instant coffee powder,
    dissolved in 2 teaspoons hot water, then cooled

FILLING
4 teaspoons coffee liqueur
120 ml (4 fl oz) double cream, whipped

1   Preheat oven to 160°C (320°F).
2   Place butter and sugar in a food processor and process
    until creamy. Add eggs and flour and process until all
    ingredients are combined.
3   Spoon batter into two buttered and lined 18 cm (7 in)
    sandwich tins and bake for 30–35 minutes or until golden
    and cooked when tested with a skewer. Turn cakes onto
    wire racks to cool.
4   To make icing, place butter, icing sugar, cinnamon and
    coffee mixture in a food processor and process until light
    and fluffy.
5   To make filling, fold liqueur into whipped cream.

6 Spread filling over one cake and top with remaining cake. Spread icing over top of cake.

Mocha Dessert Cake

Serves 6–8

PREPARATION 20 minutes   COOKING 1 hour

---

100 g (3½ oz) cooking chocolate
150 g (5 oz) butter
220 g (7½ oz) sugar
250 ml (8 fl oz) strong black coffee
1 cup plain flour
37 g (1¼ oz) cornflour
1 egg

---

1. Preheat oven to 160°C (320°F) and line the bottom of a 20 cm (8 in) round cake tin with baking paper.
2. Mix chocolate, butter, sugar and coffee in a saucepan large enough to mix all the ingredients and heat gently until butter and chocolate have melted and mixture is smooth.
3. Remove from heat. Sift in flour and cornflour and add egg. Beat with a wooden spoon until smooth, then pour the mixture into the cake tin.
4. Bake for 50–60 minutes or until cake is firm. Stand in tin for 10 minutes before turning onto a cooling rack.
5. Serve dusted with cocoa powder and accompanied with fruit.

Coffee Desserts

Here you will find a delightful selection of the finest coffee dessert recipes our chefs have devised. You will find a couple of favourites such as "Quick Tiramisu" and "Coffee Pecan Pie", plus others sure to satisfy. Go ahead and make your day with great tasting coffee recipes.

Mocha Cream

Serves 4

PREPARATION 15 minutes

---

375 ml (12½ oz) thickened cream
4 teaspoons vanilla extract
2 teaspoons instant coffee powder, dissolved in 45 ml
  (1½ fl oz) water
4 egg whites
105 g (3½ oz) caster sugar
105 g (3½ oz) dark chocolate, melted
60 ml (2 fl oz) Kahlúa

---

1   Beat the cream with the vanilla essence and coffee until
    soft peaks form.
2   Whip egg whites until stiff, then gradually add sugar and
    continue to beat until thick and glossy, about 5 minutes.
3   Combine the melted chocolate and Kahlúa with the cream
    mixture. Gently fold the egg whites into chocolate and
    coffee cream mixture until just combined. Spoon into
    4 serving glasses and top with coffee beans to garnish.

Coffee Chocolate Mousse

Serves 4

PREPARATION 25 minutes   COOKING 5 minutes

---

105 g (3½ oz) dark chocolate, melted
60 ml (2 fl oz) espresso
6 eggs, separated
105 g (3½ oz) caster sugar

---

1   Melt chocolate with espresso over double boiler. Beat the
    egg yolks and sugar until thick and pale. Add chocolate
    mixture to yolks. Beat the egg whites until soft peaks
    form. Fold whites through yolk mixture.
2   Put the mousse in the refrigerator 1 hour before serving.
    Serve with dollop of double cream and coffee granules.

Cappuccino Pie

Serves 4–6

PREPARATION 30 minutes COOKING 15 minutes

BASE
200 g (6½ oz) packet chocolate wheaten biscuits
50 g (1¾ oz) butter, melted
4 teaspoons instant coffee powder

FILLING
250 ml (8 fl oz) milk
8 teaspoons instant coffee powder
60 g (2 oz) sugar
37 g (1¼ oz cornflour)
2 egg yolks

TOPPING
2 egg whites
105 g (3½ oz) sugar
½ teaspoon cocoa powder
chocolate sticks

---

1 Preheat oven to 190°C (375°F).
2 Crush biscuits until medium-fine crumbs in a food
   processor or thick plastic bag. Pour in melted butter, add
   coffee powder and mix to combine. Press mixture into
   base of a 20 cm (8 in) springform pan or loose-bottom
   cake tin. Refrigerate while preparing filling.
3 To make the filling, whisk milk, coffee, sugar and
   cornflour together. Heat, stirring constantly, until mixture
   boils and thickens. Remove from heat and mix in egg
   yolks. Pour into prepared base.

4   To make the topping, beat egg whites until stiff.
    Gradually beat in sugar until mixture is thick and glossy,
    then spread over the filling.
5   Bake for 10 minutes or until just starting to brown.
    Dust with cocoa and garnish with chocolate sticks
    to serve.

Coffee Pecan Pie

Serves 8–10

PREPARATION 9 hours   COOKING 50 minutes

---

80 g (2½ oz) butter
75 g (2½ oz) white sugar
250 ml (8 fl oz) golden syrup
3 eggs
120 g (4 oz), coarsely chopped
1 teaspoon instant coffee powder,
    dissolved in 1 teaspoon water
pinch of salt
190 g (6½ oz) semisweet chocolate chips
125 ml (4 oz) double cream
4 teaspoons icing (confectioner's) sugar
¼ teaspoon vanilla extract

PIE CRUST
225 g (7½ oz) plain flour
125 g (4 oz) butter, chopped
75 g (2½ oz) caster sugar
1 egg yolk

PIE CRUST

---

1 Combine flour, butter and sugar in food processor, pulse
   until mixture resembles breadcrumbs.
2 Add egg yolk and enough chilled water to form a dough.
   Knead lightly, wrap in cling film and refrigerate for
   30 minutes.
3 Roll dough out between 2 sheets of baking paper and line
   a 22 cm (9 in), lightly buttered pie dish with the pastry.
   Keep the crust in the refrigerator until ready to use.

FILLING

1. Preheat oven to 190°C (375°F). In a medium saucepan, melt the butter over low heat. Stir in sugar and golden syrup and set aside to cool.
2. In a mixing bowl, beat eggs well. Stir in chopped pecans and melted butter mixture. Stir in coffee. Spread chocolate chips evenly over the bottom of the pie crust.
3. Pour pecan mixture over the crust. Bake for 45–50 minutes, or until set.
4. Cover and let stand at room temperature for about 8 hours before serving. The pie should be soft.
5. Combine cream, icing sugar, and vanilla in a small mixing bowl. Whip until stiff, then serve with the pie.

Mocha Ice Cream

Makes approximately 3 cups

PREPARATION 20 minutes

4 egg yolks
105 g (3½ oz) caster sugar
45 ml (1½ fl oz) coffee liqueur
1 tablespoon instant coffee powder
100 g dark chocolate, chopped
375 ml (13 fl oz) evaporated milk, chilled
250 ml (8 fl oz) thickened cream, whipped

1 Combine egg yolks, sugar, coffee liqueur, coffee powder
   and dark chocolate in the top of a double saucepan.
2 Stir over simmering water until chocolate has melted,
   then cool.
3 Fold in evaporated milk and cream. Pour into ice cream
   machine. Churn until firm and blades stop turning,
   approximately 40 minutes. Serve immediately or spoon
   into a container and freeze.

Tiramisu Ice Cream

Serves 4

PREPARATION 2 hours 45 minutes

30 g (1 oz) caster sugar
60 ml (2 fl oz) hot espresso
425 g (1 lb) carton ready-to-serve custard
250 g (8 oz) mascarpone cheese
100 g (3½ oz) cocoa amaretti biscuits, roughly
   crumbled
60 ml (2 fl oz) Marsala

1 Mix the sugar and coffee together and stir until the
   sugar has dissolved. Whisk together the custard and
   mascarpone until smooth, then stir in the coffee mixture,
   mixing evenly.
2 Pour into a freezer container and freeze for 1 hour or
   until ice crystals begin to form. Whisk the mixture until
   smooth, then return to the freezer for 30 minutes.
3 Sprinkle the biscuits with Marsala and quickly stir into the
   half-frozen ice cream, mixing well. Return to the freezer
   for 1 hour or until firm. Serve the ice cream decorated
   with curls of chocolate made with a vegetable peeler.

Note All the traditional elements of tiramisu are fused together in
this rich, extravagant ice cream. An ice-cream maker will cut down
the freezing time, but it's not essential.

Quick Tiramisu

Serves 4

PREPARATION 2 hours

250 ml (8 fl oz) strong coffee
120 ml (4 fl oz) Tia Maria 250 ml (8 fl oz) thickened
    cream
250 ml (8 fl oz) mascarpone cheese
75 g (2½ oz) caster sugar
24 sponge fingers
50 g (1¾ oz) plain chocolate, grated

1   Mix together the coffee and the Tia Maria in a bowl.
    Set aside.
2   Whip the cream until soft peaks form. Fold in the
    mascarpone and sugar.
3   Soak the sponge fingers two at a time in the coffee mix.
    Place into the bottom of a serving glass – you may need
    to break in half to fit into the glass. Top with some of
    the cream and mascarpone mix and sprinkle on some of
    the grated chocolate. Repeat, making two more layers,
    finishing with the cream and mascarpone mix and
    grated chocolate.
4   Repeat the process, filling the remaining glasses.
    Cover with cling film and refrigerate for 2 hours.

Mexican Coffee Balls

Makes 24

PREPARATION 20 minutes

---

250 g (8 oz) chocolate wafers, crushed
250 g (8 oz)ground blanched almonds
30 g (1 oz) unsweetened cocoa powder
75 g (2½ oz) white sugar
8 teaspoons instant coffee powder
80 ml (2¾ fl oz) coffee liqueur
125 ml (4 fl oz) golden syrup

---

1   Mix chocolate wafers with almonds, cocoa powder and sugar.
2   Dissolve instant coffee in coffee liqueur and stir into crumb mixture with golden syrup.
3   Shape into 50mm (2½ in) balls and roll in cinnamon sugar. Store in refrigerator.

Coffee Zabayon

Serves 4

PREPARATION 20 minutes   COOKING 15 minutes

---

4 egg yolks
30 g (1 oz) tablespoons sugar
60 ml (2 fl oz) very strong coffee
125 ml (4 fl oz) coffee cream liqueur
pinch of nutmeg
zest of 1 lemon

---

1   Beat the egg yolks with the sugar in a bowl until the mix
    is homogenous.
2   Put the bowl in a bain-marie where the temperature
    should be about 45–50°C (113-122°F).
3   Keep on beating the mix while adding the coffee, liqueur,
    nutmeg and lemon zest. Whisk the mix in an electric
    mixer until it becomes creamy.
4   Pour into warm goblets and decorate with whipped
    cream and powdered cocoa. This zabayon may also be
    served with chocolate ice-cream.

Coffee Charlotte

Serves 4

PREPARATION 3 hours 20 minutes

---

100 g (3½ oz) caramel sugar
1 egg
300 ml (10 fl oz) thickened cream, whipped
8 teaspoons instant coffee powder,
    dissolved in 1 tablespoon water
60 ml (2 fl oz) rum
200 g (7 oz) lady finger biscuits

---

1 Beat sugar and egg until light and fluffy. Fold in whipped cream and coffee.
2 Combine the rum with ½ cup of water. Dip the biscuits into the rum mixture, then place in a baking pan. Fill the pan with alternating layers of cream and biscuits, ending up with the biscuits.
3 Put it in the refrigerator for three hours, then remove the charlotte from the baking pan shortly before serving. Dust with cocoa and serve.

Baked Coffee Apples

Serves 6

PREPARATION 20 minutes   COOKING 30 minutes

---

6 large apples
250 g (8 oz) raw sugar
60 walnut pieces
30 g (1 oz) butter
2 small cups of strong coffee (not espresso)

---

1   Preheat the oven to 180°C (360°F). Peel the apples and
    carefully remove the cores with a core-remover, taking
    care not to damage the fruit.
2   Mix 80 g (2¾ oz) of sugar and the walnuts and use the
    mixture to fill the apple cores, then top each with a knob
    of butter.
3   Butter a baking pan and put the apples inside, upright,
    quite tightly packed.
4   Meanwhile, heat 100 g (3½ oz) of sugar and the coffee
    until they are well amalgamated.
5   Cover the apples with this syrup, then put them in the
    oven and watch the cooking.
6   Frequently collect the juice formed on the bottom of
    the pan, and pour it again over the top of the apples.
    When almost baked, put the pan on the flame, sprinkle
    with the remaining sugar, let it caramelize a little,
    and serve.

Note To make baked coffee pears, simply substitute pears
for apples.

Coffee and Ginger Almond Bread

Makes 40 pieces

PREPARATION 20 minutes   COOKING 1 hour 35 minutes

---

150 g (5 oz) plain flour
2 teaspoons good quality ground coffee
3 egg whites
105 g (3½ oz) caster sugar
120 g (4 oz) unsalted almonds or hazelnuts
105 g (3½ oz) glacé ginger, finely diced

---

1   Preheat oven to 170°C (340°F). Lightly spray or brush a
    7 x 24 cm (3 x 10 in) bar tin with unsaturated oil.
2   Sift together flour and coffee into a bowl. Place egg
    whites in a separate bowl and beat until soft peaks form.
    Gradually beat in sugar. Continue beating until sugar
    dissolves. Fold in flour mixture. Fold in nuts and ginger.
3   Spoon batter into prepared tin. Bake for 35 minutes.
    Stand tin on a wire rack and cool completely. When cold,
    remove bread from tin. Wrap in aluminium foil. Store in
    a cool place for 1–3 days – the finished bread will be
    crisper if you can leave it for 2–3 days.
4   Preheat oven to 120°C (250°F). Using a very sharp
    serrated or electric knife, cut cooked loaf into wafer thin
    slices. Place slices on ungreased baking trays. Bake for
    45–60 minutes or until dry and crisp. Cool on wire racks.
    Store in an airtight container.

Note This recipe is only limited by your imagination. You could use
any nut, dried fruit or spice you fancy. For something festive, try
cherries, mixed peel and brazil nuts, or for an exotic eastern feel
use pistachios, glacé pears and ground cardamom.

Index of coffee art

Index of recipes